EUTHANASIA

EUTHANASIA

Should We Kill The Dying?

Brian Pollard
MB., BS., DA., FFA RACS.

© Brian Pollard, 1989

Mount Series is an imprint of
Little Hills Press Pty. Ltd.,
Tavistock House,
34 Bromham Road,
Bedford. MK40 2QD
United Kingdom.

Regent House,
37-43 Alexander Street,
Crows Nest NSW 2065
Australia.

Cover design by Mary-Louise Peachey
Production and printing by Colorcraft Ltd., Hong Kong.

ISBN 0 949773 92 1

Pollard, B. J.
    Euthanasia : should we kill the dying?

    Bibliography.
    Includes index.
    ISBN 0 949773 92 1.

    1. Euthanasia. 2. Terminal care. 3. Medical ethics.
    I. Title.

174'.24

CONTENTS

1 THE SETTING   1
2 PALLIATIVE CARE IN THE LATE EIGHTIES   7
3 EUTHANASIA – BRIEF HISTORICAL NOTE   19
4 DEFINITIONS   21
5 ETHICAL/PHILOSOPHICAL BACKGROUND   25
6 REFORM OF THE LAW TO PERMIT EUTHANASIA   39
7 DISABLED NEWBORN INFANTS   51
8 OPINION POLLS   59
9 HOW MANY ARE SEEKING EUTHANASIA?   63
10 THE ECONOMICS OF HEALTH CARE   67
11 WHO IS TO DO THE KILLING?   73
12 NEED FOR HIGH STANDARDS OF
   MEDICAL CARE OF THE DYING   77
13 SOME AREAS OF DIFFICULTY   85
14 THE POSITION IN HOLLAND   105
15 WHAT LIES AHEAD?   111
16 CONCLUSION   131
   REFERENCES   135
   INDEX   139

DEDICATION

With deep gratitude to my wife Carmel, and my daughter, Lisa, who each illuminated my way along a difficult path.

1

THE SETTING

Euthanasia is now a frequent topic for public discussion, whereas it was virtually unheard of a few decades ago, except in learned or philosophical circles. The reasons for this are many, but three stand out.

First, there has been an erosion of traditional ethics with their emphasis on the transcendent value of human life. This view has been partly replaced by a secular ethic in which human life has no such enduring value and in which the moral value of a human action is judged by its perceived consequences. One result of this is that death is no longer an element in life to be confronted and prepared for. Thus, a valuable life skill to enable people to cope effectively with death, which previously was fostered in our culture and is still present in some other cultures, has become a rarer attribute.

Second, real advances in medicine have been so spectacularly successful in the treatment of certain life threatening illnesses that life can now be prolonged for many persons who would previously have died earlier. Though most wish to take advantage of this apparent benefit at the time it is offered, this decision may eventually prove for some to have been unwise and may be regretted if the quality of that extended life' has become unacceptably low. Despite professional experience, careful thought and goodwill, this outcome cannot always be foreseen in individual cases.

Third, the influence of the media, both popular and scientific, is pervasive, and it properly encourages public debate on all kinds of topics. When the issue is as complex as euthanasia, however, which stirs deep emotions in many people, these debates may be notably deficient in their ability to separate opinions from the facts on which sound opinions can be based. The result may merely be that confusion is re-cycled.

In this book, I shall try to present an objective overview of most of the important elements which make up the totality of the subject, though it would be unreasonable to expect that objectivity would equate with neutrality. Much of what is written about euthanasia fails to satisfy because of superficial or unbalanced discussion and fails to inform because it leaves the reader ignorant of many important issues. Too often, a single issue is presented for examination, a narrow view is advanced or a preconception is argued for.

THE SETTING

The main reasons why this is so include the following:

— evaluation is restricted to an intellectual approach, which obscures the humanity inherent in the actual encounter with the dying. The best interests of patients are not to be sought by considering only the philosophical arguments, important as they are. To deal with philosophical issues only is to produce an unbalanced appraisal.

— dogmatism and intemperance are regrettably common, even in the writings of some professionals, and impart a hard edge to the claimed compassion.

— the use of euphemisms which hide the real content, whether used intentionally or not. Thus, we find 'right to die' when what is meant is 'right to be killed', and a large number of expressions to avoid use of the word 'killing', which honesty would require as the only accurate description of what is being proposed, though some may find that distasteful.

— ignorance about contemporary standards of appropriate care of the dying. This leads to false arguments based on false information.

— failure to acknowledge that many of the elements, despite prolonged consideration, are difficult and unresolved.

— a presumption that the issue is capable of an all-embracing and valid answer.

Because the ethical position of a commentator will determine a good deal of what is said, it should be made clear to a reader what that position is. While my orientation is Christian, any fair minded reader will concede that that ethic has not necessarily entailed a blinkered consideration of the secular issues, and that it pays due regard to all other ethical stands. What cannot be respected are attempts to obscure the real significance of what is being proposed, or a failure to fully inform a reader, when it is felt that the information is, or should be, within a writer's capacity. Most of the issues will be treated chiefly by consideration of their relevance to the common good, public and personal morality and the welfare of individuals.

My qualification to speak is that, after a previous career spanning just on thirty years as an anaesthetist, I spent five years full time in charge of a palliative care service in a large teaching hospital in Sydney, during which time I assisted in the care of nearly one thousand patients who were dying or soon going to die. These patients and their families, as well as the best contemporary relevant literature, taught me what it is like to die and what the dying need to make this stage of life acceptable to them and their families. As a result of that experience, it is clear to me that many writers on euthanasia have no accurate concept of what is involved in dying nor of what people most need at that time.

What I am seeking to uphold is first, that it is morally undesirable and ethically unsound to attempt to legislate to take innocent human life, second, that any law which might permit this would be subject to unpredictable abuse and third, that it is socially regrettable and seriously misguided to be trying to introduce such a law at a time when modern medicine can now provide a better answer than killing to the problems which surround care of the dying. I hope that my expertise will be most useful in places where the usual contributors are most deficient. This book is not lengthy because I think a sound, but not necessarily highly erudite, guide is greatly needed by, but not available to, a wide range of persons, professional and otherwise. I have tried in each section to present the essential elements, none of which is treated exhaustively.

The subject is most often proposed as 'voluntary', that is, applicable only to the terminally ill who competently request it, and that is the context of most of this discussion. It is less often proposed for other persons who request it who have incurable, disabling diseases which are not directly threatening life, for severely deformed newborn babies or for other incompetent persons.

The motives of the supporters of euthanasia can usually only be guessed at. Without doubt, most are actuated by genuine compassion and concern and in many cases, by anger and frustration resulting from their firsthand experiences of poor quality of care of dying friends or family. A variety of understandable emotions is evident in the comments of many, though there is also evidence of a calculated indifference in those of others, an eagerness to bring a clinical tidiness into these difficult and perhaps unpleasant aspects of human life. Less often, but perhaps more important, there is increasingly to be found support for killing those whose satisfaction with their life is declared to be unacceptably low, for social, rather than medical, reasons.

The next chapter will be devoted to setting out what constitutes accepted contemporary standards of good care of the dying. This is placed at this early stage so that the reader can have this information as background during the discussions which follow. It is my contention, and one which is shared by most, if not all, of those who care for dying persons professionally, that the general adoption of such standards of care will be the most rational, most effective and most humane course of action for society to adopt, in order to answer the call for euthanasia for these people and to correct what is, in any case, at the present time, a most unsatisfactory situation from everybody's point of view.

2

PALLIATIVE CARE IN THE LATE EIGHTIES

Medicine throughout the world owes a tremendous debt to Dame Cicely Saunders who, almost alone, developed the principles of care which are acknowledged to-day as the cornerstones of good treatment in the area of the terminally ill.[1] This has been achieved during the last twenty years or so, at a time when the general thrust of medical science was vigorously proceeding in other directions. These were years of great advances in understanding of disease and in the development of new and aggressive methods of treatment of the commonest illnesses which threaten life, such as heart disease and cancer. She repeatedly and correctly pointed out that most of these advances were of little or no avail to many of the dying once a certain stage in their illness had been reached — in fact, they were then often harmful and unwarranted.

Instead, what these patients now needed was competent, detailed attention to the relief or, if possible, the removal of their physical and emotional distresses, close and warm human support, adequate honesty in imparting needed information and in determining preferences, seeking to act in accordance with their wishes, and doing all these things in the place where the patient wanted to be, as far as this was possible.

Before good care can be provided on a universal basis, we shall have to realign some of our prevailing medical goals, so that they more accurately accord with our real professional limitations and with the altered needs of dying patients, which are significantly different from those of patients whose lives are not under threat. In achieving technological progress, we have developed aggressive attitudes to treatment, so necessary and useful for many illnesses, but perhaps counterproductive for these patients. We have to become better at correctly deciding when to refrain from using common treatments which are not going to provide benefit, but which may cause further distress. Although this is not an easy part of medicine, improved performance in this area will return dividends in patient and professional satisfaction.

The components of good palliative care are:

Control of Physical Symptoms.

The great majority of patients who are regarded as having a terminal disease have cancer. While this is not the commonest cause of death, it is the disease which can carry a reasonably accurate forewarning of approaching death, and is notoriously associated in the public mind with a large number of fears, real and unreal, about its future course. Most of medicine's most powerful weapons against cancer are themselves capable of producing disability and distress, and their usefulness is generally limited to prolonging life rather than curing the disease. Indeed, a significant fraction of cancer pain is due to treatments rather than the disease. Thus, a vital part of relieving distresses, psychological and physical, is expertise in determining the appropriateness of treatments so that they are only used when they are likely to confer benefits.

Of all the distresses of the dying, pain is the most prominent and most feared. The strategies for effective control of their pain are different from those generally useful for non-cancer pain and, while the principles of drug usage in this context are simple,[2] they are not yet sufficiently widely known and not yet widely taught in medical schools. This is both tragic and challenging. Additionally, doctors are taught not to concentrate on symptoms alone, since the cause of the illness is generally the more appropriate target. For the dying, however, vigorous attention to symptom control is the right approach. When this attitude is correctly applied to all their distressing symptoms, they can be made comfortable to a degree which allows them to attend to the things they wish or need to do.

There are very few pains of cancer which to-day cannot be either totally eliminated or brought to the point where the patient can bear with the small amount of residual pain. Sometimes, this may require the help of an expert but most cancer pain is well within the competence of any doctor to treat effectively. It is necessary to regard unrelieved pain as a medical emergency to be dealt with as energetically as possible and to address also the emotional turmoil which is usually present.

Emotional Support and Communication.

Cancer is associated with anxiety, apprehensions and foreboding in most patients[3]. They are also often seriously uninformed about their illness and may be reluctant to ask. The family may be similarly placed and may feel impotent and frustrated. In the absence of effective training to meet this complex and threatening situation, doctors too may feel inept, may lack confidence and may be tempted to avoid the patient. But one who knows how to deal with this situation can produce a complete turn-about if he is prepared to take the time to calmly discuss all the patient's fears, expressed or not, answer questions, give necessary information, impart confidence, assure all parties of his readiness to be available at all times when needed, and particularly, to convey positively the idea that he or she will continue to care through to the end, no matter what may arise. Security can then replace anxiety and the patient is thus enabled to devote his mental and physical energies to achieving his appropriate goals. The doctor needs not only to convey his messages verbally, he must demonstrate his commitment by his actions.

If a doctor fails to see the importance of these functions, he may deny the reality of the patient's pain, undervaluing and undertreating it, or he may think that, since he knows he can do so little to cure, his presence is unnecessary and embarrassing, not least to himself. In reality, his presence is an essential source of strength and comfort for many patients. Despite the fact that the patient also may be fully aware of how little can be done to alter the outcome, he appreciates the support and interest and these are not less real benefits merely because they are not physical.

The attitudes of mind which enable a doctor to carry out these functions are summed up in the word empathy, an ability to place oneself in the position of the other in such a way as to be able to understand and anticipate the responses generated by the threatening situation. Empathy relates to deeply embedded components of personality, and it is commonly said that it cannot be taught or learned if the groundwork of personal experience is lacking. That is not proven one way or another, but it is apparent that the need for and the effectiveness of these strategies can be demonstrated to trainee doctors. They can be led to see that patients need and benefit from such relationships and that, if they themselves cannot provide such care, the patients' needs dictate that the doctor must find some other solution to ensure that the best treatment is not being denied them in the circumstances.

Deception, whether by giving wrong information or by witholding needed information, should play no part in the doctor's dealings with the patient at this time, though that is not the same as always telling the full truth or telling the truth in an insensitive way. The individual's needs in this regard vary from person to person and from time to time. Whatever is said must be truthful, to the extent that it meets the patient's needs, at that time. For some, this will be the full truth, if that is what is asked for, while for another, it may be a graded offering of truth which never approaches full disclosure, if that would not be welcome. The cue as to how far one should go will usually be obtained from the patient, if the signs are looked for, as one feels the way gently ahead.

The family too may need much guidance and support in this regard, sometimes mistakenly asking for deception in a vain attempt to protect the patient. On some few occasions, in some families and in some ethnic groups, this may be an acceptable course, though usually, it is better to explain that this is an unwise step which will almost certainly fail, with disastrous consequences.

Few family members are in the habit of lying to each other over important matters and, if they tried it, would rarely be convincing. Attempts to deceive are, for this and other reasons, doomed to failure. The patient may already be aware of the truth and that he or she is being treated like a child. Even when this is tolerated, it cannot be really acceptable. It is worse when the patient is not aware of the truth at first but then becomes aware that he or she has been deceived. The danger now is that trust may no longer be able to be fully given in any matter at all. Failure to disclose at least the gravity of the condition locks the family into false silence when there is, or may be, so much that should be shared while there is still time. Though the family is acting overtly to protect the patient, they themselves may be needing most protection from disclosure of the truth. If they ask for deception, they will require careful explanation of the likely outcome of that course of action, and support must then be offered to them with an assurance that the truth will be sensitively handled. In the final analysis, it is the patient's truth which we hold, and our first duty is to him or her.

The sum total of these elements is incorporated in the word communication — the two way exchange of information, feelings, attitudes and confidences. This must be an exercise in genuine human relating, as it is impossible to be false and hope to be effective. "Communication can make the difference between a composed, functioning person who is able to make the most of his life and one whose days are filled with despair ... this is a formidable responsibility."[4]

Respecting the Patient's Wishes.

A recent study of the dying in Australia[5] revealed that the common law right of every person to refuse any or all medical treatment, even that which may be sustaining life, is not widely understood by patients and is not widely promoted by doctors. There can be no question that performance here needs to be improved. To be meaningful, autonomy implies that the patients are aware, are consulted, are adequately informed about treatment options and possible outcomes, and that their expressed wishes are complied with, provided these do not interfere with the legitimate rights of others. In practice, full respect for this and other similar rights can present significant problems, for example when a patient later changes his mind or claims that he was misled, despite the best endeavours of all parties.

A good deal of criticism is levelled at doctors for the ways in which they are perceived to fail to respect patient autonomy and much of that criticism is valid. One part of the problem about full disclosure is not the question of honesty alone, but the effect which disclosure may have on the patient, at a time when he is struggling to cope with what he already knows and fears. It will often be an unduly heavy and unnecessary burden to carry on top of his knowledge of the illness and its consequences to be told in detail of the unpleasant and unwelcome effects of treatment, which in a particular case, may or may not eventuate. If they do not occur, the patient may reasonably feel he has been unfairly stressed.

I was concerned that a certain woman had not been fully informed about her plight. When I asked her whether she would want to know if she was dying, she said emphatically "No, indeed, that is for the doctor to worry about." Some will see that as old fashioned, and perhaps as an excuse for not disclosing. It is neither. It is an attitude which doctors encounter to varying degrees and which they realise would cause grave concern for the patient if it were violated. I mention it only to demonstrate that any attempt to oblige doctors to fully disclose the truth to all patients, a provision which some would want to introduce by law, would have severely damaging effects for some. The large and unpredictable variations between persons indicate that it is not as easy as it may seem to solve human problems by rule and regulation.

Self determination is sometimes spoken of as though it were the most dominant of the principles of care and as though it would be a guarantee of higher levels of patient satisfaction when people were given every opportunity to say what they wanted. Neither of these is true. As a principle, it is subject to the restraints of the competing legitimate rights of others, either as individuals or society as a whole. More important is the fact that patients will sometimes choose, with or against advice, courses of action which eventually prove to have unwelcome results ranging from merely unpleasant to disastrous.

At this stage of the illness, it is impossible to predict the exact outcome of a particular treatment. When the selected treatment does not produce the hoped-for results, and especially when it produces further distress or disfigurement, there is understandable disappointment. Now, perhaps, it can be clearly seen for the first time that the last best chance of a comfortable end to life has been missed. This can lead to recrimination and resentment, with false hopes raised and dashed again, even when the decisions were made with all due care on the part of everybody. The situation is compounded if the patient cannot accept the reality of this event and seeks a scapegoat.

Teamwork.

The skills to treat advanced cancer well are shared by several medical disciplines. The treatment to provide the best chance of eventual cure for an individual patient may only be decided after all the facts are marshalled and considered by a number of doctors, each with knowledge in a particular field. In fact, this is the standard way of approaching the treatment choice in a large hospital, to try to ensure that the best decision is made on each occasion.

While a patient certainly needs those things, they are not all he needs. Once treatment has commenced, he now needs skilled nursing to provide the comfort which will make the experience tolerable if not pleasant, together with skilled observations and judgement. In many instances, these nursing functions will be the most important elements in securing the best quality of remaining life, more needed and valued by patient and family than the medical contribution. These two groups should work as a team. Doctors need to remember that their actions determine the framework within which the nurse functions and that, failure to provide good medical care, as for example by not relieving pain, means the patient cannot receive the advantage of all that a good nurse has to offer.

This basic team may need to be increased from time to time by others, to provide, as required, special skills, such as those of surgeon, medical oncologist, radiotherapist, pain specialist etc. However large the team may become, (it needs close watching to ensure it is never larger than necessary), there always exists the need for one doctor to be seen by the patient as 'his' doctor, the one to whom questions can be directed and the one to take responsibility. Other persons may also be recruited from the ranks of clergy, social worker or other professionals. This array may appear formidable but is, in most instances, held in reserve for use in special cases, while day to day care is conducted by a small number of people who relate closely to the patient and family.

The Family.

The model for care of the dying differs significantly from that of the conventional doctor / patient relationship in that the family is now an integral part of the group, most often as members who provide care but sometimes as members who need care. The nature of the average family is such that some at least are intimately involved with all developments and their needs must also be attended to, where possible. One of the outstanding benefits of providing uniformly good care of dying persons is that the way is prepared for healthy bereavement patterns following the death.

When the patient dies, the previous events become frozen in memory. Little further can be done to change whatever happened before death. The subsequent grieving patterns of the family can be distorted and prolonged by recollection of any event about which there remains guilt, regret, anger, disappointment or other similar emotions. Remembrance of such professional shortcomings as a missed or unduly delayed diagnosis (however justified), failure to provide comfort or even to attend, uncaring attitudes and so on, are potent causes of harmful emotions. When good care has been provided, and when there was sufficient time for the parties to complete their farewells, life can be seen as having suitably concluded and grieving can proceed.

It is apparent that the standards of care for dying patients which have been described above are not those which are found everywhere at present, in their entirety. Some assume that these standards are only attainable in a hospice, and indeed, perhaps only in certain hospices. The supporters of euthanasia may claim that while it is all very well for the few who have access to such care, it is unrealistic to expect that all or most will be able to receive it.

It needs to be clearly stated that there is nothing in any of the above which is beyond the capacity of every doctor who at present has the responsibility for caring for dying patients and who has been well prepared for the task. Such skills are not the preserve of a select, highly trained few. The steps which are still required to enable all doctors to meet the needs of their dying patients to an acceptable standard are discussed in some detail in a later part of this book.

Not only is there an urgency to see the present unsatisfactory position redressed in order to relieve human suffering more effectively, but the urgency extends to the question of euthanasia. Will these things happen in time to forestall an escalation in the call for euthanasia? The answer is up to individual doctors and institutions. They must be brought to see that the common 'curing' model of medical care is appropriate for only a proportion of their patients, and that the strategies of the 'caring' model, as outlined above, are needed for the remainder who include all those whose illness cannot be cured, whether it threatens life or not. As for those with cancer, a cure rate of even 30% means that the remaining 70%, that is, the majority of those with the second commonest fatal illness in Australia, will probably have need of good palliative care at some time.

3

EUTHANASIA – BRIEF HISTORICAL NOTE

I t is generally thought that euthanasia was first put into effect on a significant scale in Nazi Germany during World War II, but the idea had been originally proposed with the appearance of a book, "The Right to Die", by Jorst in Gottingen in 1895. It was a later publication in 1920, "The Permission to Destroy Life Not Worth Living" by two authors, Karl Binding, a lawyer, and Alfred Hoche, a psychiatrist,[6] which led to wider discussion and subsequent legislation to permit euthanasia in Germany in the 1920s and 1930s. It was seen as a beneficial social innovation to deal with the useless sick, but was not racially inspired. Indeed, at that time it was denied to Jews for the very reason that it was perceived as a social advance.[7] It was practised in German public hospitals on a wide range of patients.

EUTHANASIA

At first, the stated reasons were compassion, quality of life and cost containment, that is, much the same as they are to-day. The costs of supporting the handicapped, the retarded and the insane were stressed ('useless eaters'). Eventually, by the late 1930s and early 1940s, the indications had expanded to include those with minor defects, the senile or war veterans, no longer on request, but at the initiative of doctors as 'mercy killing'.

It was later in 1939 that Adolf Hitler formally signed it into wider use, and this led to the later excesses of human experimentation and genocide. The way had been prepared for such developments by doctors, lawyers and clerics who had espoused the practice earlier, in contravention of their professional obligations and undertakings to respect all human life. It is a matter for serious reflection, with modern parallels, that this happened in this way and that those doctors who participated in the later episodes of genocide were all volunteers.[8] What started as an attitude about the disposability of the non-curable sick quickly grew into something much more sinister.

4

DEFINITIONS

The terminology of the debate about euthanasia can be confusing, so some definition of terms is necessary. The word 'euthanasia' to-day implies that there is an intention to bring about death, either by doing something or by omitting to do something. The commonest terms are:

A. active, also called direct.

i. voluntary. This refers to patients who are mentally competent, and who ask to be killed in order to relieve distress, either physical or emotional, which they declare to be intolerable. In response, somebody would kill them, with intent. This would be homicide by request. The usual setting for discussion is in relation to terminal illness but other patient groups may be included also.

ii. non-voluntary. This refers to patients who cannot give consent, for any reason, and includes
   a. the senile or the intellectually handicapped,
   b. disabled newborn infants. These would be examples of homicide by the agreement of parties other than the subject.

iii. professionally assisted suicide.

B. so-called passive.

There is confusion about the use of this term. If it is to be defined as 'deliberately inducing death by the witholding of treatment necessary to sustain life', then any such practice would be the moral equivalent of active euthanasia, by omission rather than commission. This would be so whether the treatment was simple, such as the provision of food and drink by the normal routes, or sophisticated, such as a respirator.

The more usual context is where treatment is ceased because it is too burdensome and/or because it is of no benefit, either at the request of the patient or in the best judgement of the doctor, or both, but where there is no intention to take life. This includes various kinds of treatment but rarely refers to life support treatments, because such methods are generally inappropriate for these patients and hence rarely used on them. Thus, when discussion about euthanasia concentrates on the cessation of life support treatments, it is not dealing with the common situation.

In its common medical context, the term is a misnomer,

in that it refers to medical practices which are ethical and, when properly performed, constitute good medical practice. They are declared by some to have special significance in this setting because, since the patient is already dying, he may, though does not always, die soon after. These practices are:

a. deciding to discontinue treatment which has failed to benefit the patient and which may even be adding to his troubles. This decision may be at the discretion of the doctor or at the request of the patient.

b. deciding not to commence treatment which it is judged will not benefit the patient.

c. using vigorous measures to control severe distress, usually pain, even though they may possibly shorten life. This is often so misrepresented that it is inferred that virtually every time a doctor uses strong analgesics in adequate dosage to properly control pain, he is secretly inducing death. In reality, severe pain can be and almost always is relieved by doses which have no direct influence on length of life. If length of life may be compromised by doses which are required to control pain, humane medicine, supported by the law, demands that they not be witheld. This was repeatedly affirmed as good medical practice in Australia by the Victorian parliamentary inquiry, mentioned earlier[5].

In its usual medical context, therefore, passive euthanasia is a misnomer because it is neither passive nor euthanasia. In the face of the inevitability of the situation, these practices represent the pursuit of the patient's best interests, either to procure necessary comfort or to avoid the unnecessary and unwanted prolongation of the act of dying. They are not passive because they require the continuation of every valid, necessary form of support and treatment to ensure physical comfort and mental ease throughout the remainder of the illness, no matter what may arise. They are not euthanasia because they are not done with the intention of killing, nothing is done to kill and they are not the cause of the death which may or may not follow.

Doctors should resist the efforts of the supporters of euthanasia, who are commenting on aspects of patient care which are outside their field of expertise, to re-define legitimate medical practices, so that it appears, or can be made to appear, that doctors already do things to kill. It may happen that some doctors do sometimes secretly kill dying patients, from compassionate motives. It is often claimed that this is so, but without any evidence which can be tested. If this is the case, it has nothing to do with the practices which are being discussed here, and to confuse these circumstances displays either ignorance or mischief. It would be absurd to suppose that secret killing takes place in hospitals on any scale, possibly supported by the silence of colleagues, nurses and administrators. A moment's reflection should affirm that.

The literature of the pro-euthanasia societies contains these errors. This blurred distinction can be, and then is, used by them to justify what may look like the small extra step to intentional killing.

5

ETHICAL/PHILOSOPHICAL BACKGROUND

When they hold to any developed philosophy, the advocates of euthanasia are usually utilitarians, of one kind or another. Utilitarianism was developed in the last century as a reaction to the traditional religious philosophies which had the central concept of God as the creator of man, who was then responsible to God for his life and had an obligation to abide by God's revealed commandments. With the erosion of a transcendent view of life, new ways of determining such things as the moral value of a person, the morality of an individual's actions and the moral regulation of society had to be found.

Utilitarianism.

Utilitarianism denotes a group of philosophies, with differing emphases,[9] but with the common premise that the morality of an action is determined by evaluating its outcome, that is, if the outcome is good, the action was good. This was the method adopted to replace the existing alternatives, with their reliance on authority and absolutism. By the new approach, it was hoped man should be able to gauge the morality of each action on its merits, rather than by recourse to a predetermined set of rules, in the making of which he largely had no say. Individuals were thus freed to follow their own interpretations of morality, and could produce an almost infinite spectrum of opinions. The most rigid of this group are the adherents of Jeremy Bentham, the Benthamites, but many utilitarians follow him in some places and go their own way in others. When considering the words of a utilitarian writer, it is impossible to know precisely what views in detail that author holds, so the following remarks must be regarded as generalisations, as they may apply to an individual.

Bentham's theme is paraphrased as seeking the 'greatest good of the greatest number', where good is most easily equated with happiness. This philosophical approach appeals because it looks as though morality can be individualised to a particular action. Difficulties soon arise when one tries to define or to measure happiness, to say whose happiness will prevail when there are competing interests, which is almost always the case, or to say when the good of society prevails over the good of a person. Much greater difficulties attend the assigning of moral values and priorities to different life forms.

Here is a statement of this philosophical method from Barbara Smoker, a humanist and utilitarian who is in the forefront of the advocacy of euthanasia in the UK. She says

ETHICAL/PHILOSOPHICAL BACKGROUND

"In humanist thinking, there is no such thing as an absolute principle: various principles compete for pre-eminence according to their relevance in the particular circumstances of the case and to individual priorities".[10] Apart from the irony that the first part is itself an absolute pronouncement, the remainder of the statement can only mean whatever one wants it to mean. And this is the most important observation to be made about this form of utilitarianism – it means what one says it means because one says it. Bentham was right because he said he was and one's personal interpretation of morality is right because one asserts it.

Seen in this light, utilitarianism can be used as the ultimate hedge against the harsh necessity to be morally responsible for one's actions. When morality is asserted to reside in the outcome of the action, and if I am now both judge and jury as to what constitutes a good outcome "in the particular circumstances", I can usually absolve myself of responsibility for adverse outcomes. This is truly flexible philosophy. The traditional philosophies require a person to face up to the consequences of his intentions, for good or ill, as does the law, where intent is the essential determinant of guilt. But if one wishes to shed notions of personal guilt to the greatest possible extent, utilitarianism can supply the method. What might have looked like an advance towards the avoidance of absolutism, has come to the position where a morality is replaced by a myriad of moralities.

Contrast with other codes.

Legal and ethical codes, including those of medicine and religious philosophy, hold that the right, and therefore the power, to take the life of a dying person does not lie with other persons and that therefore, euthanasia is unethical. The World Medical Association[11] and the British Medical Association[12] have reviewed this position within the last year, in the light of contemporary practices, and have reaffirmed their stand. But burdensome treatment which may be prolonging life may be ceased, and the patient will be, and must be, afforded all care and comfort to minimise or eliminate distress for the remainder of life. A euthanasiast says that that is not good enough – if the patient wants to die, it is a matter of moral equivalents whether the patient is killed with intent or is allowed to die. (Incidentally, to state the choice in that form, as is usual, is a potent example of intellectualism. The expression 'allowing to die' conceals, and hence suppresses, the enormous scope of human relationships which may be entailed over a considerable period of time following such a decision, as outlined in chapter 2. The cessation of active treatment is not the cessation of care, which is now continued under what may be particularly trying and deteriorating conditions. The term 'allowing to die' gives the impression of cold decision making and nothing more.)

If utilitarians assign equal moral responsbility to direct killing and letting die when the intention in each case is to take life directly, either by commission or omission, there can be no dispute about that. They are equally morally reprehensible actions, and forbidden by law. Confusion arises, however, when two different classes of action are being compared, one where there is an intention to take life and the other where there is no such intention. The latter is commonly but incorrectly described as euthanasia by those who disregard the intention and look only at the outcome.

ETHICAL/PHILOSOPHICAL BACKGROUND

Consider two doctors, each dealing with different terminally ill patients, who have each expressed a wish to die. In each case, death is ultimately inevitable, only the timing can be changed. One doctor, perceiving that the treatments being used are both burdensome and ineffective, ceases them and then provides, together with other carers, all requisite physical and emotional support until the patient dies. The other doctor, perceiving the same factors, gives his patient a lethal dose of a drug. By utilitarian definition, the outcomes are claimed to be morally equivalent and good because the patient in each case is dead, as he wanted to be. In order to reach this conclusion, the intentions of the two doctors have to be ignored, as playing no part in the moral assessment. That is, the traditional most essential measure of assessing morality, namely intention, is set aside, and the morality of each doctor's act is assessed only by the degree to which it conforms to the expressed preference of the patient. If it is to be seriously claimed that the morality of one's actions is to be predicated solely on their accordance with the wishes of another, on what does this claim rest, beyond unsupported assertion?

In the above example, what has become of the doctors' autonomy, by which they themselves may assess the correctness of their actions and of their responsibility to act according to that judgement? The first doctor in the example above did not intend to kill, he did not perform any act of killing, either by commission or omission, death followed his action but was not due to it, and yet, by utilitarian principles, he is now deemed to bear a moral responsibility equal to that of killing. To be upheld, this concept requires a rejection of virtually all existing legal and moral codes.

And what would be the morality in utilitarian terms of a

decision to let die when the decision had been ill judged, whereby the patient, after the treatment was ceased, now improved, rather than proceeded to die? This does sometimes occur, since medical judgements are by no means infallible, and the course of illness cannot always be accurately predicted. Now the outcome may be deemed morally bad, since it is not what the patient wanted. If the doctor was previously judged to have carried out a good action because the outcome was morally good when he killed on request, of what bad action can he now be accused, when the patient did not die? Is he guilty of not killing?

Use of euphemisms.

The expression 'allowing to die' creates difficulties, no matter how it is defined. Literally, it would imply that someone had the power to prevent death and did not do so – in the case of terminal illness, that is never the case. For some, it is a euphemism for killing. If it means 'allowing the illness to run its natural course', then that may be different from allowing to die, since death may not follow as a consequence.

More profound difficulties arise when utilitarians consider the moral value of human life. The usual way in which they approach this task is to give arbitrary credit for grades of developed human attributes. Thus, some will say all sentient life (that is, life which has the capacity to experience pleasure and pain) has equal value, putting animal and human life at the same moral level[13]. Some will place higher emphasis on intellectual abilities, the highest of all being related to the ability to be self aware and perhaps to take responsibility. For some, only the presence of such developed characteristics can justify the description 'person'. These approaches have the result that human life is now given varying values as between individuals and at varying stages of normal or pathological life. Infants, the feeble and the retarded score low values on such scales. Some of the practical significance of these assessments will become clearer in later discussion on killing disabled infants.

By what means are such assessments of life value made and how are they to be validated? They are ultimately based on personal opinions and "various principles" which "compete for pre-eminence according to their relevance in the particular circumstances of the case". They are validated by assertion only. There may be as many answers as there are commentators. There are no agreed answers to such questions as "what is life?", "how do we come to possess it?", "in what sense can it be said that our lives are our own – do we in fact own them as we own other property, do we inhabit our life or are we not sure what the statement may mean?"

Since we are all ignorant in many important ways about the most fundamental aspects of life, what can be said about taking decisions regarding the disposal of human life, when such decisions have unknowable consequences? Is the subject not one with such inherent possibilities that every aspect demands the most careful evaluation lest the outcome be regretted? Christians are often chided for trying to influence the public morals of others and accused of arrogance for their efforts. At the very least, a custodianship over that which is not well understood has the advantages of a suitable awareness of one's limitations and a suitable caution.

Strict utilitarians, like the Benthamites, do not acknowledge the existence of any human rights whatever[14]. This is a difficult stance for any person or group to maintain, at variance with what virtually everyone instinctively and rationally regards as part of his human entitlement, held dear by him and protected by the law. It is watered down, therefore, in practice by individual utilitarians. Conversely, not everything which is claimed as a right is in fact so. The notion of rights, in general and in particular, requires considerable attention and reflection. There are different kinds of rights, some regarded as fundamental, applying to every person and deserving the protection of the law to safeguard the safety and peace of all, and others which are less potent or less general, with which the law may not concern itself. For example, if I am weak, you are obliged by law not to take advantage of that to injure me, but you may not be obliged to help me, though I may feel I have the right to both of those.

The supporters of euthanasia frequently claim it as an exercise of one's 'right to die'. A right may be defined as a claim we have on others to do something or to refrain from doing something for us. Although it has a fine ring to it, there is no such thing as a right to die. The concept of a right to an action which is universal and inevitable is a nonsense. Rights exist or they do not, they are not manufactured by claiming them, nor can they be manufactured by any authority which proclaims them if they do not already exist. The law can properly only protect such rights as exist and which may need protection.

There is a right to life and there is a right to life with dignity while one is dying. The latter may be described as the right of dying persons to call on society to assist them in their dying and to relieve them of suffering and distress by every valid means available. That right places an obligation on others to respond by meeting those needs. This right and its corresponding duty are upheld by common law at present and can be augmented by specific laws to strengthen them, if thought necessary.

As it becomes increasingly apparent that proper care of the dying is based on respect for a number of valid human rights but that these are not sufficiently well promoted or known about, changes in the law have been introduced to guarantee their observance. In Australia, this has occurred in two states, in recent years. In 1983, in South Australia[15] and again, in 1988, in Victoria[16], laws were enacted to draw specific attention to the right of every person to refuse unwanted medical treatment. In Victoria, there is further provision to protect the professionals who observe these rights against possible subsequent vexatious legal suits. In neither case, is euthanasia the issue at stake, nor is it referred to in the legislation.

What the advocates of euthanasia are, in fact, claiming is not a right to die, but two different rights, namely the right of some to be killed on request in certain circumstances, and the right of others to respond to that request by killing them. The right to be killed and the right to kill do not exist in our society and they are not established merely by asserting them. The advocates have so far preferred to use the gentler phrase which, intentionally or otherwise, hides the substance of their proposal. For honesty and clarity, they and every other person who discusses euthanasia should desist from this use of 'right to die' and be required to produce some evidence or argument for these other rights, if they wish to continue to claim them. Certainly, this should be done before submitting any case for law reform. One cannot expect the law to be radically changed to protect that which does not exist.

In passing, it may be noted that the law says nothing directly about rights; it deals mainly with duties. It indirectly upholds rights by defining and regulating the obligations on society which stem from the most obvious of the agreed rights. If it is claimed that there is a valid right to be killed on request, then it should oblige compliance. Can this be upheld?

But not all the adherents of euthanasia are humanist utilitarians. Most pro-euthanasia societies count clergymen among their membership, including some in prominent positions. A recently republished book written in support of euthanasia contains chapters contributed by such people[9], though some of these contributors wrote their material a long time ago. It can be assumed that they also are motivated by charity and compassion, as they see it. How this is to be reconciled with the injunction "not to kill", or as some would phrase it "not to do murder", is their own affair. Some who have discussed their moral attitudes reveal an alignment with utilitarian principles. Some are merely muddled and simplistic. Most, however, argue along lines like these: spiritual beings have the right to use intelligent control over physical nature; man has reason, freedom, conscience and the possibility of ordering his own life — these attributes should be used to choose when faced with an evil which has no remedy.[17]

Christians need to acknowledge that their religion, like every other, does not have the final answer to many of the current relevant questions related to dying. What religion does is provide a given framework within which one has to try to discern a solution to moral dilemmas, respectful both of the perceived claims of God and the genuine rights and responsibilities of humans. Theological attempts to re-examine the fullness of the nature of persons are in progress in many places to try to see to what extent those lives which may be a parody of this fullness may diminish, in some part, the concept of a fully alive person. It can be confidently stated that most theologians are alive to the disastrous consequences which any deviation from the principle of the inviolability of innocent human life would have. Prudence should caution against ill considered attempts to preempt such deliberations, while, in the meantime, putting all one's energies into seeing that suffering is alleviated to the greatest possible extent.

Role of suffering.

The role of suffering is difficult to discuss in such a way as to define a distinct area of common ground. A minority will emphasise suffering as an integral part of life which ought to be accepted as such. The majority believe human talents should be exercised to reduce suffering to a minimum, though to try to eliminate it altogether would be impossible. There is a middle position which holds that suffering has a positive, optional role in the development of a self disciplined human being, and that, acceptance of such an attitude can, within limits, enhance character formation and spiritual formation. In other words, some suffering can be beneficial. Most people agree with that, and can acknowledge that they would never have achieved some of their personal strengths without at least some trial by fire. How this is to be applied to the condition of the dying is an individual challenge.No universal principle can be drawn.

Opinions on suffering should not influence patient care. If suffering, physical or emotional, can be mitigated and the sufferer wishes this to be done, then it must be done to the limits of contemporary ability. Some of the emotional accompaniments of dying, such as sadness, cannot be removed. Despite that, it is a common experience that, as families work through the last stages of living together, even though there may be difficult or unpleasant elements, the parties experience real growth in their relationships and their characters. This sometimes occurs to a quite unexpected degree and to unexpected candidates, who now come to treasure the experience as a precious, rewarding, even joyful, occasion. Such emotions are a valuable resource for the forthcoming bereavement.

While there is no possibility of the reconciliation of philosophical difference, opposing viewpoints deserve respect, even when they seem false. It will have to be enough to state the differences clearly so that individuals are aware of their origins and substance, and their other possible consequences, as will be discussed later.

Proponents of euthanasia identify the churches as their main opponents and, among them, the Catholic Church in particular. These groups are labelled as conservative, standing in the way of attempts to substitute a new set of flexible principles for those which the believers in religious philosophies regard as given to all persons for their proper functioning, and not open to change by them. Why should Christians, it is objected, want to impose their own sets of standards on the community? Why not leave others to determine what they prefer for themselves which is, after all, 'voluntary' euthanasia?

ETHICAL/PHILOSOPHICAL BACKGROUND

This reasoning seems perfectly valid and has been used by Christians through the ages as they sought to obtain their just rights. But they, and any other person or group who identifies with their position, are entitled, perhaps even bound in conscience, to oppose proposed changes in the law which they perceive will have moral and social effects which will adversely affect them, despite claims to the contrary. They see that a society, which would legally sanction the taking of innocent life, supported by claims based on assertion only and which, as will be seen in a later chapter, would be a likely precedent for unpredictable extension into unforeseen areas, had reached a stage where those fundamental principles no longer apply which had hitherto ensured the security of all. That would be to be gravely disadvantaged. If such opposition is interpreted as wishing to impose a viewpoint, then that is a misstatement of its nature and purpose.

The final observation in this chapter concerns a question which needs to be, and will be, put in a variety of contexts. Why the emphasis on killing? The protagonists in the debate must know (and if they do not, their claim to credibility is undermined) about the potential of modern palliative care to alleviate the suffering of the dying, with the possible exception of a very small number. Why then is killing, to meet the expressed wishes of a few, considered better than lending support to raising the standards of care of all who are dying? Not only would large numbers now benefit from improved care, but it could be predicted with certainty that many, if not most, of those patients who now consider euthanasia would then feel no need to do so. Why would any person continue to advocate lawful killing while neglecting, even in some cases being contemptuous of, efforts to remove the most potent cause of the felt need to be killed?

6

REFORM OF THE LAW TO PERMIT EUTHANASIA

The law in respect of killing is clear and unambiguous. The unlawful killing of a person is homicide. Whether that amounts to murder or manslaughter depends on the intention; homicide committed 'with malice aforethought' is murder. The law applies equally whether intentional death follows acts of unlawful commission or omission. Euthanasia, properly understood, is a form of homicide.

Although attempts at suicide have been decriminalised, assisting in suicide remains a criminal act in all but a few legislations. This apparent split in thinking, whereby it is a criminal act to assist suicide but not to attempt it, has led to the claim that both actions should be legally 'equal', and not criminal matters. This is based on the false assumption that non-criminalisation is an equivalent of legal endorsement.

EUTHANASIA

The real interpretation is that the law on attempted suicide is framed to provide mercy, not approval, in a context where penalties are not only inappropriate but do not serve any proven deterrant function.

With relevance to euthanasia, the reason why attempted suicide attracts a merciful legal response is because it is recognised that such an act can be reasonably presumed to be the product of disturbed thinking, of some sort. The law is entitled to suppose, in the absence of contrary proof, that the same consideration may apply to requests for euthanasia.

The domestic criminal law of homicide is reinforced by international obligations and commitments undertaken by those governments which are members of the United Nations.

Article 6 of the International Covenant on Civil and Political Rights,[18] provides that:

"Every human being has the inherent right to life. This right shall be protected by law. No one shall be arbitrarily deprived of his life".

The U.N. Declaration of the Rights of the Child[19] states:

"The child shall have the right to adequate nutrition, housing, recreation and medical services". Principle 4.

"The child who is physically, mentally or socially handicapped shall be given the special treatment, education and care required by his particular condition". Principle 5.

In the U.N. Declaration on the Rights of Mentally Retarded Persons,[20] it is stated:

REFORM OF THE LAW TO PERMIT EUTHANASIA

"The mentally retarded person has, to the maximum degree of feasibility, the same rights as other human beings".

The U.N. Declaration on the Rights of Disabled Persons[21] provides:

"Disabled persons shall enjoy all the rights set forth in this Declaration. These rights shall be granted to all disabled persons without any exception whatsoever and without distinction or discrimination".

By aligning itself with the principles contained in these declarations, the state publicly supports measures directed to the protection of the life and welfare of its citizens. It may define exceptions for the public good, such as for the protection of its citizens from aggressors, and such exceptions may be particularly necessary for its most vulnerable members. Equally, the state has a compelling interest in opposing any moves which would undermine those rights and, by the above declarations, accepts an implied obligation to do so. It would be a profoundly significant step for a signatory state to legislate to remove such protection, though it be for compassionate reasons, and it would be necessary to ensure that any consequences of change did not infringe the rights of other persons. As will be discussed below, this would probably not be possible.

Common law.

It is also the common law right of every person to determine what treatment he or she will have for themselves. The right extends even to treatment which may be sustaining life but which is regarded as too burdensome or is offering no benefit, where such treatment may be seen as doing no more than needlessly prolonging dying. This right is not adequately known about by patients and is not adequately promoted by doctors, but the Medical Treatment Act 1988, recently passed by the Victorian Parliament in Australia and dealing with intellectually competent patients, endorses and delineates it. The Act provides for the exercise of the right following adequate provision of information to enable the person to make an informed choice and rests a legally binding obligation on the professional attendants to respect and abide by such decisions. By some, it is considered regrettable that the other provisions of the bill, regarding the clarification of the rights of incompetent persons, were not proceeded with. These could have given legal status to advance declarations and could have helped decision making in some difficult situations. It is to be hoped that this omission will be soon corrected.

Reform of the domestic laws relating to homicide would be the first step to the introduction of legal voluntary euthanasia. While the law is often criticised for its conservatism and for lagging behind public opinion and community acceptance, it responds that this is not necessarily a bad thing, in that hasty, poorly thought out decisions are minimised which, once in place, may be impossible to reverse. Additionally, and especially when the issue is complex, public opinion may be ill informed and may thus be the basis for bad law. Euthanasia is primarily an ethical problem, rather than a legal one. The law regards social ethical problems as being best dealt with by social measures wherever possible, without recourse to law where this can be avoided, and expects that the community will have done its ethical exploratory work first, as discussed above regarding rights. It may then decide to enshrine change in the law, if it is convinced that the principles and practices which the community seems to want will benefit from the protection which the law can provide. It is important to reflect on this function of the law and upon the fact that rarely, if ever, is new law made by courts. By and large, courts apply the existing law and such new laws as parliament enacts.

To date, attempts to reform the law to allow legalised euthanasia have not met with success in any part of the world, with the possible exception of Uruguay, though some supporters of reform predict that it is only a matter of time before the legal barrier will be breached. It is possible that this could occur because of a powerful lobby rather than because the legal principle was perceived to be overwhelmingly supported. It could also happen as a result of confusion about terms and practices in this difficult area. Confusion is already widespread, both because of inherent difficulty with the subject and because of its intentional creation by those whose personal interests will be best served by confusion. This could occur in a country without a tradition of high standards of legal practice, in a country with different kinds of legal processes or in a country in which the law was traditionally looked to in order to resolve ethical problems, rather than allowing society to fully define and debate the issues. A wedge effect could then follow elsewhere.

Public opinion.

Since law makers may be shown to be at least partially

responsive to public opinion, it follows that those who would not welcome any adverse change in our present law regarding homicide, should, as a matter of urgency, take an active, informed interest in the debate on law reform. This would entail a program of reading, discussion and, when opportunity presents, the making of a reasoned case for alternative practices with medical and social benefits which are as great as those which it is claimed would flow from euthanasia, but without the need to change the law to allow killing. In this way, public opinion may be helped to develop along lines which protect the valid rights of all persons.

It also means, for medical and nursing professionals, self education about current palliative care practices and their widespread adoption by all those with any responsibility for care of the dying. This should be accepted as a humane obligation, whether or not there is a question of reform of the law to enable euthanasia.

In the United Kingdom, Australia and Canada, attempts have been made over the last twenty years to reform the law to provide for euthanasia or mercy killing. During such a review by the Law Reform Commission of Victoria in 1974, it was observed "it is not practicable to devise any (re-) classification (of mercy killing) that will not be subject to the gravest criticism. Further, any classification of degrees of murder based on relative heinousness must necessarily be extremely unsatisfactory and productive of anomalies"[22].

The most recent review in Australia occurred in Victoria in 1987, when the Social Development Committee of the Parliament of Victoria made its report on *Options for Dying with Dignity*. This document should be read by every doctor who treats the dying. Its findings are treated more fully in a later chapter, but, specifically, the inquiry rejected one of the solutions which had been recommended to it to relieve the sufferings of the dying, namely euthanasia, when it concluded "it is neither desirable or practicable for any legislative action to be taken establishing a right to die"[20]. This may be one of the last occasions on which doctors and the community in Australia will be offered such a straightforward, clear sighted blueprint for a positive, ethical strategy to redress the medical imbalances which have arisen here, as they have in every other Western nation, as a consequence of an unreflective embracing of medical high technology.

In the United Kingdom, three bills were unsuccessfully introduced into the parliament between 1936 and 1969, and the Criminal Law Revision Committee undertook a review in 1976, during which the arguments for and against euthanasia were well evaluated[24].

In 1983, the Law Reform Commission of Canada recommended, following an inquiry, that 'mercy killing not be made an offence separate from homicide'[25].

Why Law Reform Attempts Have Failed.

The reasons why all these previous attempts at law reform have failed need to be considered. While they are instructive, they are no guarantee that such would receive comparable weighting in any future consideration, in any country. The elements which have been the most difficult to resolve are the following:

    — the motive of the person performing the act. This would

be exceedingly difficult or impossible to determine accurately. The claim of compassion, as the most likely motive, could not be objectively tested.

— possible error of diagnosis or prognosis.

— meaningful descriptions of intolerable distress. These have had to be made complex in order to allow for every contingency and as a result, have been subject to a myriad of interpretations.

— the most difficult of all was the matter of the consent or dissent of the patient. The law has been unable to be explicit in defining the patient's complete freedom and competence to make an unambiguous choice, free of all external influences. In the emotional environment which surrounds dying, there may be possible degrees of fear, anxiety, mental confusion, paranoia, depression, coercion or feelings of worthlessness which cannot be detected, let alone measured.

These factors may act powerfully but subtly to influence choice, and there have been many reports which strongly bear this out. It is not an uncommon experience for patients to make what seem at the time to be definite statements of intent, only to retract them as definitely some time later. They are subject to fluctuating moods and opinions, just like everybody in crisis, and may later be quite distressed at the thought that anybody may have taken them seriously. A well known example of this is the case of Mrs. Bouvia in the US.[26]

It is refreshing then to note that some ardent and thoughtful advocates of euthanasia who previously supported reform of the law have acknowledged that there are inherent, significant difficulties with this, not yet resolved. Lord Raglan, the proposer of the 1939 Bill in the UK, later said, after hearing the full debate, that he could no longer envisage adequate legal safeguards for all and that, in any case, there would be no need for euthanasia if terminal care was everywhere brought up to the standards he had seen in the hospices[27]. Dr. Raanan Gillon, a prominent British ethicist and supporter of law reform for euthanasia for many years, said in 1986 that after the most mature reflection, he did not now know in what way, if any, he would want the law changed[28].

Other commentators have thought that, although the present legal position may not be satisfactory from a number of viewpoints, every proposal for change so far advanced has also been unsatisfactory in important ways. In view of the constraints which the law has imposed on the practice of abortion and the ways in which those constraints are now widely disregarded in Australia and elsewhere, (reminiscent of the situation in Holland regarding euthanasia, where the law prescribes it as a capital offence but it is widely and openly practised), there could be little confidence that reform of the law to allow voluntary euthanasia would be able to be restricted to that practice. If close study in many places over a considerable period of time has not thus far enabled a satisfactory law to be framed, it would appear likely that any future law would be flawed and inadequate for its purpose, unless some breakthrough can be devised to solve the impasse.

Potential for abuse.

Once the principle that self determination of the limits of acceptable tolerance of distress was an approved reason for some to be killed and others to kill, a proposition which would be incapable of being tested objectively, it would be difficult, and probably eventually impossible, to refuse it to others in comparable degrees of distress, not necessarily medical. While nobody would impute motives of widespread social engineering to a majority of the supporters of euthanasia at the present time, some do not hide the fact that their eventual aims extend further than the terminally ill, once public opinion has been conditioned to killing as an acceptable mode of dealing with this social problem. This is more fully discussed later.

The lawmakers have generally been able to appreciate these concerns, to see that a can of worms would be opened by a law change. In reality, all the consequences could not be calculated in advance and it will be dishonest for the advocates of euthanasia to dispute that. They emphasise that they merely want change for those who ask for it. The law has repeatedly maintained that it would be impossible to devise a law which would protect the rights of all parties and which could be restricted so as to apply only to the group under discussion.

The Law Has Its Limitations.

When the law points out that it is incapable of determining precisely either the motive of the one intending to do the killing, or the capacity of the person asking to be killed to freely and competently choose, it is saying it would be powerless to detect or prevent abuse. In that case, the rights of all persons to their life could not be guaranteed and the outcome would be unsatisfactory and, possibly, dangerous. Non-lawyers are not fully competent to evaluate all these distinctions, but we would do well to proceed with caution.

Given this background, it is not good enough for the supporters of euthanasia, and especially professionals who may be expected to be more constructive in their thinking, to continue to press for unspecified law reform, as though these reviews had not taken place and as though it would be a simple matter if only we put our minds to it. They should acknowledge the valid impediments which have been uncovered, and as a further rational exercise, should suggest, if they can, legally sound proposals which might overcome the difficulties. These could then be debated publicly.

7

DISABLED NEWBORN INFANTS

Killing disabled newborn infants is generally referred to as infanticide. In Australia, infanticide is the precise legal term for the killing by a mother of her infant, in certain circumstances, so, in this discussion, the above term will be used for clarity.

It is important to treat this topic, which was defined earlier as a form of euthanasia, at some length, as it contains two elements of great importance.

A Utilitarian View on the Value of an Infant's Life.

The first is that the school of bioethics which is leading the philosophical move for euthanasia in Australia has a special interest in this subset of the subject, having published and spoken widely on it. The Centre for Human Bioethics at

51

EUTHANASIA

Monash University, with Professor Peter Singer as director and Dr. Helga Kuhse as assistant director, promotes a secular humanist philosophy of utilitarian orientation which underpins the position of all the organisations which are working for the legalisation of euthanasia. These commentators are also noted for their pronouncements on animal liberation. Their views regarding the moral value of the life of animals and of humans, particularly that of the newborn human infant, with or without deformities, need to be understood in order to evaluate their proposals.

They dogmatically reject the Judeo-Christian tradition as being controversial and a myth. They credit it with being responsible for our 'hang ups about killing' which they think we shall have to learn to master. They ignore the fact that their proposals are at odds with every code of ethics, medical and legal, and at odds with universally acclaimed declarations of human rights.

In the context of killing certain of the newborn, their philosophy, which it may be recalled is based on arbitrary definition and assertion throughout, proposes a range of values of life, both human and animal, which is related to and dependent on individual developed characteristics, rather than on the fact of the individual's being a member of the particular species. At the lowest level, all lives which are capable only of experiencing pain or pleasure, are said to have equal value, whether they are human or animal. To be credited with higher value, lives must possess "at least at a minimal level, the capacities distinctive of the species which include consciousness, the ability to be aware of one's surroundings, to be able to relate to others, perhaps even rationality and self consciousness"[29].

Only these lives are then gratuitously accorded the status

of personhood. They are the only ones who are defined as persons and who merit the rights which attach to being a person. The fact that the authors do not specifically refer to rights is beside the point. Such are implied and every reader will so interpret their writing.

Therefore, "no infant, defective or not, has as strong a claim to life as beings capable of seeing themselves as distinct entities, existing over time"[30]. This statement sets out the opinion that the value of the life of an animal may be higher than that of any newborn infant. Further, "killing a defective infant is not morally equivalent to killing a person"[31]. This statement declares that, having arbitrarily defined the infant as a non-person, it would therefore be a lesser evil to kill it than to kill an adult.

And finally, "this conclusion is not limited to infants who... will never be rational, self conscious beings," ... "everything I say about them would apply to older children or adults whose mental age remains that of an infant"[32]. These statements complete the circle of arbitrary definitions, to the effect that a person of any age who is mentally incompetent to a defined degree, by virtue of that mental incompetence alone, is similarly declared to be a non-person, and so, may be killed more lightly than any other person of that age. It is difficult to see what social purpose such arbitrary redefinition of terms serves other than to make the destruction of certain infants and persons less reprehensible, if there exist other reasons to want to do this.

Normally, a person may be defined as "a human being, whether man, woman or child".[33] But this philosophy claims that the defective infant does not have the moral value of a human person, nor does any other retarded human, child or adult. It is, therefore, the ultimate rationale not only for their killing as individuals, but for the extension of the application of the principle to the region of eugenics. One commentator wryly observed that, by such criteria, the infant would have difficulty qualifying for an I.D. card but could easily get a death certificate.

Occasional Paper No. 10 of the Australian Human Rights Commission – A Comment.

The second element which requires comment is the Occasional Paper No. 10 of the Australian Human Rights Commission on "Legal and Ethical Aspects of the Management of the Newborn with Severe Disabilities", published in 1985[34]. It states in its introduction that "its purpose is to raise key issues and arguments associated with this subject in order to encourage public discussion". Despite the facts that Australia is a pluralist society and that the Commission is publicly funded, the panel which prepared it contained no person active in the pro-life interest, but did include Dr. Helga Kuhse, a proponent of direct euthanasia. In light of its sponsorship, it could have been expected that it would put views protective of human lives, especially those of the handicapped. This it did not do.

The Paper does not follow a logical sequence whereby the presentation of alternative arguments is succeeded by their explicit assessment and a synthesis of relevant aspects. Rather, it is discursive, anecdotal and given to opinions. Its thrust is to support euthanasia for deformed newborn babies, to advocate amendment of the law to recognise a new class of (non) persons who may be put to death at the authorisation of a group of experts because they fail to meet certain arbitrary criteria. It goes so far as to prescribe a procedure for deciding which (non) persons fall within that class, and a draft model law for the latter purpose is included as Appendix B which would allow parents to request the killing of their defective children up to the age of 18 years.

There is not even a mention of the fact that such law might be inconsistent with, or contrary to, any human right recognised or declared in international conventions and declarations, as set out in the Human Rights Commission Act. The presumption, based on normal human behaviour patterns, that, were an autonomous act of choice possible, the infant would probably wish to avail himself or herself of the ordinary standards of human and medical care, is set aside.

The Paper makes use of the common trick of the euthanasiast, namely the resort to euphemism. One of its compilers referred to infant killing as "helping the handicapped child not to survive". It quotes, without dissent, a paper by Dr. Kuhse which advocates "a quick and painless injection" for an infant with Down syndrome and oesophageal atresia (a deformity which prevents swallowing), without discussing the possibility of surgical correction of the blockage, the standard operation for such a deformity.

It can thus be seen that these philosophers and the compilers of the Paper just mentioned would deny basic human rights to the most vulnerable groups in our society. Since they are the same philosophies and philosophers on which and on whom the supporters of euthanasia rely in Australia, the latter are now publicly aligned with those whose policies favour eugenics, the killing of the unfit for the improvement of society. Whether they are aware of this connection and whether they are comfortable with such an association is not clear. But it is difficult to claim that one supports only half a philosophy.

Disabled Newborns – Specific Considerations.

Singular elements are present in the case of disabled newborn babies which are absent when adults, even incompetent adults, are being considered. These may be stated as:

a. the impossibility of determining the actual preferences of the subject,
b. doubts in some cases about the prognosis, i.e. can the infant survive and if so, for how long?
c. for those who will probably survive, the unknowability in many instances of their quality of life, and
d. most distressing emotional components for the parents in many if not all cases.

The grossest physical deformities which are incompatible with any significant length of life do not cause much trouble with decision making as those infants soon die. Difficulties arise when the deformities are not threatening life and may not do so for years, if ever, but when in somebody's view, the person is likely to have a poor quality of life. Although its frequency cannot be known, the practice has grown up in a proportion of such cases for the parents, usually after counselling, to decide that the infant is to be deprived of nourishment and thus caused to die, and for the staff to carry out those wishes. In the United Kingdom, it has been testified that these practices are common, even routine in some places.[35]

Two things can be said about this – first, there can be no doubt that by such practices, some lives are taken which would have been no different from those of many living individuals who enjoy a quality of life which is quite acceptable, and often very dear, to them and their families and second, it is expressly forbidden by current law.

While there can be no question about the great mental anguish which these decisions cause, not only at the time but possibly, for the rest of the lives of some of the parties, the present situation is obviously most unsatisfactory. Flexible philosophies regarding the value of human life can accommodate to such practices and offer a solution, which is said to be compassionate. They also make it easy to avoid what in some instances will be no more than ordinary parental responsibilities, no greater than those which have to be faced by many or even most parents regarding their children at various times later in life. That consideration cannot be regarded with equanimity by any person. The case where parents agree to or request death by 'benign neglect' (how benign is an action with a 100% mortality rate?) when the deformity is or may be compatible with a tolerable life, can be reasonably described as death on request for a social reason. It would be as logical to wait to see whether the parents could cope and if they could not, to kill the child later. If that is a repugnant thought, it can only be because the principle behind the action has been clarified.

The ethical stand that innocent human life is not for mankind to dispose of may demand of ordinary people in these circumstances levels of courage which some possibly do not possess as individuals. If that were the case in a particular situation, it would be wrong to force compliance on the parents. The resources of the rest of society would, however, be more than adequate to meet the challenge if it had the will, either to support or in extreme cases, to replace the parents for a period of time, which in many instances would not be of great duration.

8

OPINION POLLS

There are reasons to have reservations about opinion polls which purport to show significant public support for euthanasia. Some of these reasons are:

a. since the terminology is confusing even for experts, there can be little confidence that poll respondents interpreted the questions only in the ways in which the pollsters thought.

b. emotional accompaniments are always present with this subject, playing an unknown part in supplying an answer without reflection.

c. misunderstandings of medical practices and their proper roles are so common as to be virtually always present in a subject group, to further obscure the replies.

d. it would, in fact, be very difficult to frame the questions in such a way as to guarantee truly informed replies from an unselected group.

e. the well known propensity of respondents to give a misleading answer when they are not faced with the actual dilemma seems to be borne out by the fact that, when terminally ill patients are provided with large quantities of drugs for pain control, more than enough to be lethal, as is now common, they virtually never take advantage of this opportunity to take their lives.

Two significant questions were included in the much quoted Morgan poll in Victoria in 1986[36]. The first asked, in essence, 'should the terminally ill have the right to choose to die?' 86% answered 'yes' but there is no way of knowing how many respondents quite reasonably interpreted the question as a reference to the right to choose that their illness be allowed to run its course, rather than that they be further subjected to unwanted treatment. For that indeterminate number, the question was not about euthanasia at all. The other question asked, in essence, 'if a terminally ill person asks for a lethal dose or asks for some other help to die, should that person be helped to die?' 74% of respondents were in favour. But how 'some other help' was interpreted and how many thought it meant no more than the provision of palliative care cannot be known. (The Victorian parliamentary committee, for example, took it to mean the latter[37]). Despite such glaring imponderables, the poll was widely claimed as showing 'enormous' and 'overwhelming' community support for euthanasia. Such unwarranted conclusions can only be described as tendentious and misleading.

More recently, a poll of doctors' practices and attitudes was published by Drs. Kuhse and Singer.[38] Similar flaws are apparent in it, attributable, in part, to its use of euphemisms for killing and in part, to its questions which are framed in inadequate ways. Again, it cannot be known whether the respondents interpreted the questions in the way the pollsters thought. This is a most misleading poll since it was inaccurately directed to an important group of professionals, whose reliable answers could have been very helpful concerning their practices.

Its misuse of language is such that the expression "assistance in dying" in the article refers solely to direct killing! In one place, it states "as long as assistance in dying cannot be given openly, it will not be available equally to all." Apart from the fact that real assistance in dying is already given openly everywhere to the dying, this quote can be accurately interpreted thus: "as long as we cannot kill people openly, we will not be able to kill all those who have been so poorly cared for, or who have so poorly prepared themselves for their inevitable death, that they are driven to ask to be killed." It is true that the highest standards of assistance in dying are not yet available equally to all, but that is partly because some of those professionals, who should have the best interests of dying persons at heart, campaign only for their destruction rather than their good care. A result of this is that when the necessary quality of care has not been generally available, the proffered solution for some is death.

Having said that, it is also true that the public is now more ready to discuss the topic than previously and more ready to assent to it. There is a perceptible loss of interest in religious practice and precept so that the proposal does not encounter the moral objections it may once have. There are too, increased levels of medical consumer awareness and articulation of viewpoints, though these are no guarantee of increased understanding.

It is reasonable to ask 'on what basis of information and evaluation are the answers to public opinion polls likely to be grounded?' to try to be sure that the poll results do not merely reflect significant ignorance about a complex issue. Members of the public will have obtained their information and, in many instances, their opinions from the media, with few exceptions. The acknowledged aims of the media are to sensationalise and titillate, in order to make sales or foster controversy. Rarely do they set out to supply a balanced treatment of a difficult and complex subject with the object of increasing knowledge and awareness, and it must be said, they are rarely equipped to do so. And if they did, how often would it be fully grasped? Additionally, can there be any confidence that the abandonment of religious adherence has been replaced for most by an alternative, reasoned ethic which will enable them to make considered moral assessments? And even if such assessments were valid, is the moral worth of an argument to be judged by the number of those who subscribe to it?

Such observations do not make it seem likely that the answers to opinion polls, even those directed to professionals, are soundly based on either information or understanding of the issues.

9

HOW MANY ARE SEEKING EUTHANASIA?

It is not possible to supply estimates of the numbers of persons for whom legalised euthanasia may be sought. The impression is given by its supporters, though, that they are numerous. Why else would such a drastic step as law reform be thought necessary and hard fought for, if it were not considered that this was the only way to correct a widespread social evil? My extensive personal experience would utterly refute such an impression. In five years of full time care of the dying, the great majority of whom had advanced cancer, not one patient asked for euthanasia, although the service which I directed attracted some of the most complex and challenging medical problems. They included common and uncommon complications of an illness, cancer, which is notable for the range of difficulties which it may present.

EUTHANASIA

A few patients discussed euthanasia at some stage of their illness, usually to satisfy themselves that it was not on the agenda for them, but sometimes to indicate that, if things became intolerable at some time in the future, they would want it. They were always told that, if things should come to that pass, they were to raise the matter again, and they knew they would be listened to. Nobody did so. The concern which was far more commonly expressed was that they would have their lives needlessly and inappropriately prolonged and it was most important to assure them that that was never done on that service and that their lawful requests would be adhered to, invariably.

The Family.

The people who not only discussed euthanasia but sometimes suggested it for a particular patient were the relatives or friends. It is not sufficiently appreciated that the family may and often does suffer more than the patient. They are not receiving concentrated attention yet they may have much the same kind of fears, anxieties, anger, frustration and feelings of impotence as the patient. They may cope less well, especially if there is unresolved guilt regarding the dying person. Their request for euthanasia is a form of saying "please put him out of my misery". Nobody could imagine, let alone claim, that euthanasia would be any kind of solution to such an unfinished human event. Rather, it would ensure that the unfinished business would never be resolved, to remain a source of anguish, perhaps for all time. The only real solution to this challenge is to try to define the elements of the problem for all those involved and provide support for them to face the difficulty as well as they can while there is still time.

I cannot claim that, if I had continued in that work for a longer time, I may not have been asked by a patient or patients for a quick and easy death. But if that had occurred, it would almost certainly have been for reasons of emotional distress and exhaustion and not on account of physical pain. What my experience and that of every other doctor who practises palliative care reveals is that if the dying are well cared for, they have little need to ask to be killed. The corollary holds that if they ask to be killed, it is likely that they have been neglected, though there will be a small number to whom that does not apply. My recurring question needs to be put again at this stage. Why the emphasis on killing the dying instead of accepting the challenge, admittedly sometimes difficult, of caring well for them? At the least, since any of us may be a prospective candidate for such care, why not press for a better deal from which one may possibly benefit personally?

It is easy to give the impression that there is a large pool of patients who would want to be killed, if killing were legally available, but there is no evidence to support that. Conversely, the evidence from those involved in this work is that it is much more likely that the concept is promoted by suffering by-standers who are responding to individual instances of poor care, or by those who wish to see the answers to social problems in philosophical terms alone, for their own reasons. Every observer will agree that some change is urgently needed in the way we care for the dying, but the loudness of the call for euthanasia is not a measure of its basis in fact, nor of the need for that kind of change.

It has been suggested that the prevailing ambience of

total care and support which is found in a good palliative care setting could inhibit a request for euthanasia. The patient might refrain from asking for it out of consideration for the obvious good will of the staff and so, no requests do not indicate that there is no need. One cannot have it both ways. Is anybody seriously suggesting that in hospices and other places where good palliative care is being provided, there is possibly a significant group who are so distressed that they are contemplating being actively killed, but nobody is aware of it? There will always be a small number of patients who will express such thoughts from time to time, but they are usually giving vent to general feelings of discontent with what is happening to them. This is entirely normal in the circumstances, and is rarely consistently maintained when openly explored. If there is any real doubt that terminal care can be as good as its practitioners claim, the evidence is there to be tested by anybody who wishes to do so.

10

THE ECONOMICS OF HEALTH CARE

For some time now, commentators have foreseen a potentially difficult time in the future, when the community may no longer be able to afford to care for all such groups as the aged, the mentally incompetent, the gravely injured with little chance of returning to productive life, the grossly deformed and perhaps, the dying. A natural reluctance to discuss the economic aspects of these issues would be understandable, though not necessarily rational. It could appear that a monetary value was being placed on a human life.

The population in Australia for instance, is ageing at a rate which sees the number of persons over 65 years increase by about 54,000 per annum. The skills of medical technology ensure that more persons can now be kept alive longer than previously, though that is not necessarily in the best interests of society, individuals or doctors. Changes in patterns of disease are also occurring with distinct economic consequences. For example, the death rates from both heart disease and stroke have been almost halved in the past twenty years, but those who live longer as a result are surviving to develop cancer in greater numbers.

It is ultimately neither possible nor desirable simply to ignore matters of cost and economics. If they are not brought out into the open, decisions may be taken in ways which are hidden from public view or accountability, perhaps using criteria which are unacceptable. Where the dying are concerned, it may be impossible to distinguish moral from economic arguments, unless all parties are given the opportunity to examine the proposals and their grounds. It has been suggested that openness in discussing the costs of medical care as a principal reason to introduce euthanasia would have the effect of rendering it likely that such a proposal would never receive public support, but there could be no certainty about that.

It would be illogical and unfair to single out any particular group of sick persons for scrutiny on the basis of costs incurred. Who might, then, be considered, in practice? Some criteria would have to be decided — would they include those with the least likelihood of return to productive life or those who incurred the greatest medical costs? Would it be those whose bargaining position was so weak that they would make the least noisy objection or might a health budget for the year be struck, with danger for any group after the deadline was breached? If those suggestions are seen as macabre, as indeed they are, how might it be done? Would there be the slightest chance that there could be a financial proposal based on any truly humane considerations?

Warning signals have already been detected in the ways in which some now refer to minority or disadvantaged groups in the community. A prerequisite to attempts to move against any such group would be to discredit it and lower its social value in the public eye. For example, the repeated use of derogatory expressions about ethnic groups or the young unemployed can be used to prepare the way for placing blame on them for the social burdens which they represent. Such methods are not in common use about dying persons at present, although the previous discussions about the disabled newborn are not entirely reassuring, but they could be invoked to deprive them of a sense of social worth. This would act powerfully to prepare them and others to accept the solution of euthanasia to what may have become a significant economic dilemma. In this regard, the dying are a particularly vulnerable group, only too prone to feelings of worthlessness which, in many instances, need strong countervailing efforts to dispel. Unless society had sound moral values regarding the worth of this group and was willing to back those values with action, the way could be open to their exploitation by moves to kill them for reasons of expediency.

Another Possible Outcome?

The supporters of euthanasia would be rightly affronted by any suggestion that what they propose can in any way be linked with eugenic doctrines and no person imputes such motives to most of them. But the link is not as tenuous as

they may have convinced themselves. The earliest proponents of euthanasia in the US admitted that such was indeed
their logical ultimate intention,[39] – the clearing away of the
burdensome detritus of society. Further, some of the present supporters of euthanasia freely admit that their proposals can be logically extended to any person who feels overcome by the weight of life's pressures, and that legal killing
could be extended to them and to those who, from certain
philosophical viewpoints, are deprived of their full entitlement to respect as persons. To draw attention to the possibility of uncontrolled and unexpected applications of a
principle of lawful killing is not fanciful. Indeed, there is no
way in logic that expanded applications could be resisted,
and compelling economic arguments may become the
stimulus to do so at some time in the future.

In looking to contain escalating health costs, some
avenues could be explored, without violating any moral
principles. One of the most contentious areas is that of
intensive care units, in which many die though such
patients are not, by the usual definitions, terminally ill. The
following have been suggested, therefore, as areas in which
economic components could be objectively considered
now, yielding information on the costs of supporting the
dying:

a. the development of better criteria for admission to intensive and critical care units,
b. wider promotion of patient and family autonomy regarding decisions to refuse treatment,
c. a critical examination of the present costs of caring for
   the dying in different settings and
d. the effects on such costing of provision of subsidies to
   enable more persons to be cared for in their homes.

THE ECONOMICS OF HEALTH CARE

Option c has already had some attention devoted to it. It has been established, in Australia and elsewhere, that the cost of caring for the dying in their homes is not less than that of hospital care, when the costs of the necessary community services which may be required to assist the home carers are taken into account. This reflects present methods but there may be scope for economies of scale if home care were to be undertaken for more patients. The advantages of home care may be centred on patient, family and community satisfaction and quality of care rather than on costs, since many patients and their families nominate home as the preferred place in which to die, whenever that is possible and feasible. But the stress placed on caring families in this situation, even with adequate assistance, should not be underestimated.

11

WHO IS TO DO THE KILLING?

T his question is an inescapable detail of euthanasia. It is not often openly discussed, and the tacit understanding is that doctors would do it. Until recently, their views on this had not been sought. The way in which it was done, however, was such a clumsy one that it is impossible to draw reliable conclusions from it.[38] Doctors appear to be as divided as the rest of the community, and their opinions may be as unsupported by an acquaintance with all the issues as prevails elsewhere.

Should doctors be the ones to carry out the killing? The reasons why they may be thought to be the most appropriate are that they will be the ones who were involved in the medical assessments of incurability, they would have to provide the certification and they might be expected, after a close relationship throughout the illness, to know the patient's true state of mind. A reason of lesser quality is that they have the neatest, most acceptable means to hand. But none of those factors bears directly on any exclusive responsibility, whether offered or accepted, for the act of killing.

The proposal of doctors to be killers is at odds with their traditional role as the trusted group to which society has given charge of its life and health. The ethics of medical practice are directed to the upholding of those things. Killing persons whom they cannot cure has never been part of the doctors' commission.

A number of factors have arisen in recent years, conspiring to foster a deterioration in the quality of doctor/patient relationship, at least in public. Two of these are an improvement in medical consumer awareness and articulation, and a realisation that doctors have not been well prepared by their formal education to deal well with a range of illnesses which rely heavily on an empathetic bond between doctor and patient. This deterioration is not regarded as a beneficial development by any of the parties. Rather, it is regretted all round, with many trying to devise ways of reversing it to restore the provision of uniformly good care. Anything which may cause a further falling away can be expected to be a retrograde step.

The patient groups which have suffered most from these deficiencies are those for whom secure, trusting relationships are most necessary, based on confidence and competence in caring rather than curing. These are the most difficult and demanding skills to acquire and to provide, and the dying are probably the best example of those who most need them. Would an environment of security be helped or hindered by a perception, perhaps a distorted perception since virtually everything in medicine can be poorly understood, of doctors as killers? Would not the knowledge that euthanasia was available to cover the inadequacies of poor treatment be likely to act as a disincentive to strive for higher standards of care? The number of ways in which awareness of the availability of euthanasia could influence patient, family, medical and societal attitudes is large indeed.

Those who have given the matter considerable thought have concluded that the medical profession would be well advised, at a practical level, to have nothing whatever to do with euthanasia. There would be no necessity for doctors to take any role in any of the proposed processes of killing, which would essentially be expressions of a contract between an individual and society. Doctors would have little to gain and much to lose by becoming involved. If that advice is to be accepted, who then might be proposed instead, and under what circumstances? Advocates might be expected to have a prepared position on this, so that the totality of their proposal can be discussed.

12

NEED FOR HIGH STANDARDS OF MEDICAL CARE OF THE DYING

The components of good care in this context were outlined in an earlier section of this book. Their place in the medical spectrum now needs some further elaboration.

Whatever one says or thinks about euthanasia for the terminally ill, the focus of attention must ultimately be on the circumstances and the quality of their medical care. Practical solutions are not to be sought or found in the halls of theology or philosophy, no matter how necessary and helpful they may be in defining and refining guidelines. The solutions are to be found, if they are to be found anywhere, in hospital wards, in homes and in medical schools. In an ideal world, care for all would be such that no person would need to contemplate the need for euthanasia. We ought to be able to agree that it would be a massive disaster to legally allow the killing of sick patients unnecessarily.

So, we can look first at the prevailing standards of care of the dying and then look at what may be regarded as the highest standards attainable. Where there is any discrepancy, then we can look at ways in which this may be reduced to the greatest possible extent, mindful that it will never be possible to do this completely in any field of human endeavour.

The most recent survey of prevailing standards in Australia was carried out by the inquiry of the Social Development Committee of the Parliament of Victoria, Australia into Options for Dying with Dignity, and its results were published in its final report in April 1987.[5] Although its findings were made within the context of law and procedure in Victoria, there is no reason to suppose that a similar inquiry elsewhere would have found significant differences. Widespread deficiencies of care were revealed in a number of areas of this work, notably in poor control of terminal pain, in lack of effective communication and the offering of human support. This finding accords with the experience of those who work in this field and reflects the inadequacy of past and current medical education to prepare graduate doctors for dealing uniformly well with these patients.

That Committee had the proposition put to it that a solution to these inadequacies was to legalise euthanasia. It specifically rejected that proposal, however, and took a more positive view because it saw that, while euthanasia may relieve the unhappy situation for some, it would do nothing to prevent others from finding themselves in the same plight at some time in the future. Among its 31 recommendations, it strongly urged the universal adoption of the principles and practices of modern palliative care by all professionals with any responsibility for the dying and it called on medical educators to introduce urgently such teaching at an effective level in all medical schools.

The Unfortunate Dynamic.

The present unfortunate dynamic can be accurately represented as follows: inadequate medical education leads to inability to relieve pain and other distress, which then leads to unnecessary suffering, which leads to further calls for relief, which leads finally to a perceived need for euthanasia. This being the real sequence of events, killing the failures, by concentrating attention at the end of the line rather than at the start, would be a bankrupt solution, calculated to ensure a continuation of more inadequate care. The only responsible course for a society which wishes to address the problem genuinely is to start with the elimination of the cause.

It is easy then to decide, on the evidence, that we need to do better. But the solution will be more complex than may be supposed. The reason why there is a call for euthanasia at this time is partly related to the nature of modern medical practice and its shortcomings. That is, we are having to deal with factors which did not previously exist.

It needs to be well understood that examples of unacceptable standards of care may be occurring despite the best efforts of doctors, in many instances. The advances of medical science have placed in their hands methods of treatment which are powerful against disease while being uncertain in their effectiveness, but powerful also in their capacity to produce their own measure of distress. Surgery, radiotherapy or chemotherapy must often be used if cancer is to be effectively treated, but when they don't produce a cure and perhaps make things worse, then we may have converted a tragedy into a disaster, despite the best judgements having been used. Present knowledge is inadequate to enable doctors to be able always to predict more accurately precisely who may benefit from advanced treatment. In these circumstances, the way forward is not clear.

Not only will we need to develop some new skills in these difficult areas, and this may take considerable time, but we need also to re-think some of our attitudes about treatment, particularly when patients cannot be cured. The objectives of treatment for these patients are different from those which applied at an earlier stage of their illness, and it is important that treatment is, as far as possible, appropriate to their needs at every stage. What might be these changed criteria for 'appropriate' treatment when cure is no longer possible?

A multi-disciplinary group from a number of hospitals in the US, when considering such criteria, concluded that, for incurable patients, two stood out: 'Is it what the person wants?" and 'Will it make him feel better?'[40] These criteria respect autonomy and direct attention to comfort but they do not accord well with those in common use. If we look at the tragic medical case histories which are advanced as justification for the need for euthanasia, they are almost invariably found to be examples of abuse, sometimes gross abuse, of patients' rights to information or choice, or examples of medical mismanagement or neglect, judged by today's best standards. We can reasonably conclude then that they could have been avoided by the use of the above criteria and of current best treatment plans, and that, as a result, those arguments for euthanasia would have disappeared.

We readily see the removal of a patient from a method of treatment which has become burdensome or useless as an ethical issue, and sometimes it is. What we may need to see more clearly is that to commence such treatment in the first instance, was perhaps just as much an ethical issue, because if it was inappropriate, it was bad medicine. When a treatment can best be described as prolonging the act of dying, unless it has been competently requested, it is inappropriate. A recent writer had this to say: "Ideally, modern health care is seen as a shared process, a partnership between the professional who is an expert on medical matters, and the patient who is an expert on what he or she wants."[41]

Medical Education.

The availability of legalised euthanasia would have profoundly adverse effects both on standards of care of the dying and on medical education. This work is often sad and difficult and there are already enough disincentives which naturally and understandably draw professionals away from it. Where would be the incentive to strive harder for the best possible care or to educate for those standards of care if the way was open to avoid the issues altogether? It may be hoped that most would not give in to such temptation, but it would be, undeniably, easier and cheaper to kill than to care well.

The primacy of the role of medical education has been referred to several times. The necessary up-dating has to take place in medical schools, hospitals and colleges and be undertaken by individuals, in order to ensure that the achievement of change is not needlessly delayed. Throughout Australia, there are now established palliative care services in teaching hospitals in some States, nurse directed services in many country regions, medical specialists fully engaged in this work as a career, and trainee positions for those who wish to be trained for such in the future. The degree of development and organisation of these services varies from State to State, but even the best of them still need to be extended. There is also available now comprehensive, inexpensive literature specifically devoted to the subject, suitable for the instruction of every kind of doctor and nurse who must provide this form of care.

Palliative medicine is concerned with the study and management of patients in whom the prognosis is limited, and the focus of care is on their quality of life. It has been regarded by some as a 'soft' subject, more suitable to nurses alone and not worthy of the skills of highly trained doctors. This is to misread seriously the doctor's real role for the many for whom cure is not a valid goal. For these patients, most of the advances of modern medicine have no further relevance. Instead, the patient, his family and the other members of the team need the correct diagnosis and prescribing, wise decision making, accurate information, leadership and confident human support throughout the illness which draw on all the talents of the well trained doctor, who can now meet the needs of all his or her patients, not only those who will recover.

The recent appointment of a full Professor of Palliative Care at Flinders University, Adelaide, an institution which is rightly regarded as a centre of medical educational excellence, should lend some necessary impetus to the incorporation of this discipline into the mainstream of orthodox medical education and care.

13

SOME AREAS OF DIFFICULTY

In this section, a number of different elements in the spectrum of terminal care and related illnesses, with relevance to euthanasia, will be examined. Their common link is that they contain areas of doubt or difficulty, where there are misunderstandings or ignorance or, as yet, perhaps no practical solutions at all. The order in which they are discussed has no significance.

Misunderstandings about Pain Control.

A frequently given reason for proposing euthanasia is unrelieved pain, though it is sometimes referred to as 'unrelievable' pain. The latter expression is not justified unless the patient has already been treated by every best strategy currently known to medicine. The following information is therefore included in the interests of accuracy and so that every person may have a genuine appreciation of what they may reasonably expect for themselves or others, in the circumstances. Too often, unacceptable standards of care are tolerated because it is not known that better standards are available.

The control of the pain of terminal illness occupies a properly prominent position in the minds of patients and professionals alike. Unfortunately, among both groups, there are misconceptions which unnecessarily increase the fear which is already present or stand in the way of successful treatment. It cannot be too strongly emphasised that the following primary statements are ALL UNTRUE, and the true position follows the statement in each case:

    – *all cancer is associated with pain.*
About one third of cancer patients experience no pain or moderate pain.

    – *the pain of cancer always gets worse as the illness progresses.*
It is quite common for such pain not to progress at all or to do so only slowly.

    – *cancer pain eventually becomes so severe that it cannot be relieved.*
This should not be true except in the most rare cases – 'unrelievable' pain is often only what somebody has not been able to relieve. Expert care will abolish or relieve virtually all cancer pain.

    – *if medication is started too early, it will lose its effectiveness.*
This is one of the really damaging myths which prevents

patients from taking, and professionals from prescribing, adequate medication at the right time.

— *if pain killers are taken regularly, the patient may become an addict.*
This is a common reason for poor medication. It is a quite unjustifiable fear.

— *pain killers should only be taken when pain is present.*
The best way to use pain killers for cancer is first, to abolish the pain, and then, take further REGULAR doses BEFORE THE PAIN COMES BACK. It is important to realise that this may mean taking pain killers when no pain is actually present.

— *morphine is only used when the end is near.*
Morphine is in common use now, started when the doctor thinks the severity of the pain requires it; its use has nothing to do with the stage of the illness.

— *injections are needed to control severe pain.*
Most cancer pain can be controlled throughout most of the illness by pain killers used by mouth or by suppository.

— *pain control is always associated with drowsiness.*
Though drowsiness is commonly present at some stage of the use of pain killers, this usually passes off and the person can continue to function adequately. If worried by drowsiness, one should speak up so that changes can be made.

— *modern pain control is so good that all cancer pain can be abolished.*
Some cancer pain cannot be completely abolished, though

it can always be lessened. Restricted physical activity may be necessary to achieve this.

— *regular use of pain killers will shorten life.*
It is not common for pain killers to have any effect at all on length of life. They may sometimes shorten it but just as often will extend it. Their correct use is not any form of euthanasia.

— *one must put up with pain as part of life's burden.*
It is a person's right to refuse medication, but, in the presence of severe pain, this attitude will result in much unnecessary suffering, not only for the patient but also for those who are living with or caring for him or her.

The effective control of cancer pain, using modern principles, will do more than any other single measure to raise the quality of life for the dying person, the family and other carers. Unrelieved pain should be seen as a medical emergency. If pain is not being relieved by ordinary measures, further professional help should be sought.

Do We Need Heroin to Control Terminal Pain?

The call for the legalisation of heroin to control the pain of terminal illness is based on a misunderatanding, similar to that behind the call for euthanasia itself. In both instances, it is incorrectly assumed that the present unsatisfactory state of affairs represents the best that modern medicine can achieve. So, it is said 'let us have heroin because other pain killers are inadequate to control pain', and 'let us kill the dying because there is no better way to control their distress, whatever it may be.'

At the outset, it must be clearly understood that where

there is inability to control pain with morphine, it is almost always on account of an inability to use it well, and that is the result of defective medical education. While there is such prevalent ignorance of the principles of good pain control, the availability of a new drug would mean one more drug to be used unwisely. Both drugs are narcotics, and when morphine, properly used, is ineffective, so would be heroin. Not all pains, even when severe, respond to narcotics.

Heroin is a man-made derivative of morphine, whereby chemists have made a small alteration to its formula. When heroin is administered to a patient, this modification is reversed within a few minutes by chemical action in the body which converts it back to morphine, and it is as morphine that it acts as the pain killer. In due course, it is morphine, not heroin, which is excreted in the urine.

In the UK, where heroin has always been legally available in medicine, the standard drug used by mouth to control terminal pain is still morphine, in hospices, in hospitals and in the community. When injections must be used as, for example, for patients who can no longer swallow, heroin is preferred. This is solely because it is physically much more soluble in water than morphine, so that the volume of the injection can be kept small, an important consideration for the comfort of patients who may be emaciated. This same advantage can be had with morphine in Australia, since it is supplied here in a more concentrated form than is available in the UK.

Since heroin has not been legally available in Australia since 1953, there are almost no doctors here with practical experience of the drug, so in trying to assess our need for it, we must turn to those elsewhere whose experience is contemporary, relevant and extensive. Dr. Robert Twycross, a prominent hospice physician and one of the foremost pain researchers in the UK, says there is no known advantage of heroin over morphine as a pain killer and no reason why any country, which does not have legal heroin, would need it to control terminal pain adequately. What is needed is the ability to use morphine, other drugs and other strategies more effectively.

This is also the experience of those doctors who treat the dying in Australia on a full time basis. If there were any advantage to be had from heroin, it would be they who would most feel the need for it, but they are not among those who call for it because they know it would offer no advantage.

Even if heroin is no better and no worse, it may be asked why not make it available for those doctors and patients who want it? Since it is already a drug of widespread abuse, associated with a significant incidence of crime, there would be problems of personal and property security in places where it would need to be stored, such as hospital pharmacies, and, particularly against such a background, it would be both illogical and potentially dangerous to do so. If it were ever in the future to be proven to be a superior drug, then those cautions may need to be reviewed, for the sake of good patient care. It is a separate but related question as to whether legalised heroin should be available to drug abusers.

The Control of Emotional Distress.

The more perceptive commentators correctly note that this may be a more intractable problem than pain control.

SOME AREAS OF DIFFICULTY

Throughout life, individuals learn how to cope with threats to their welfare, well-being, security, bodily integrity and finally, their life by meeting and overcoming the challenge in all such circumstances. The psychological coping mechanisms are essentially the same in kind in each case but may differ in degree. However these skills are acquired, they will ultimately become part of one's behaviour patterns. While most learn, some do not, and for different reasons. Some avoid the issues, leaving them to a capable spouse, for instance, or they deny their reality, and instead, keep deferring the problem.

When inevitable death has finally to be faced, whatever skills have been learned during preceding life are now mobilised and augmented by the loving support of families and friends. For most people, this is enough. But what of those who have not learned? It has been said that it is as little use to try to acquire these skills on the death bed as it is to learn marital skills on the marriage bed. They have two alternatives. They may do what they have found so effective on so many occasions before, namely deny the reality of the event and carry on as though it were not happening.

It can be difficult for those who have not encountered this phenomenon to appreciate how commonly it is invoked and how effective it can be in helping solve the patient's problem. It can be invoked as a prop to be used occasionally, varying in intensity and from time to time, or it may be a main component of coping. This denial can, in some instances, be continued right up to death. It does not of course solve the family's problem of impending loss, in fact it usually aggravates it, because dying is now not a legitimate subject for open discussion. Such persons could never be candidates for euthanasia, because in their stated view, they are not dying.

The alternative response is to remain in a state of irresolution, enduring varying degrees of anguish and not as a rule able to take full advantage of whatever support is offered. These people are most unfortunate, and while they are not common, they are sufficiently common to be the focus of a great deal of discussion and frustration. Unlike those who were in pain, they cannot always be helped, if they lack the essential skills, since no other person can do the adaptation for them. The dilemma facing euthanasiasts is whether such people, who may be regarded as the hard core of the case for euthanasia in the terminally ill, need reform of the law to enable them to be killed, on request. Their need is hardly medical, it is more nearly social. If the law is to be reformed for them because they have not learned a life skill, then surely, there can be no case whatever in logic for witholding killing on request from other social casualties who ask for it.

It is a relatively new idea that unhappiness should not be as much a part of the human condition as happiness (however one may define these terms). Life always was and will always be an amalgam of good and bad, happy and unhappy. It is immature to suppose or hope that life should only contain its pleasant aspects — a kind of childish longing for the impossible. The task of social engineering in order to try to bring this about is not only doomed to failure but discounts the notion of a fully adult human being as one who shares the burdens as well as the rewards of life. Those who cannot manage it alone deserve all our assistance. But if killing is to be applied for their relief as a last resort, we have become parties to the fantasy.

Dr. Admiraal, a Dutch anaesthetist who frequently carries out euthanasia in Holland, seems to be more aware than many of his colleagues of the true plight of this group of patients. He acknowledges what most pro-euthanasia advocates miss entirely or are loath to admit. " 'Pain' related to depression, fear and sorrow should be recognised as an alarm signal, indicating shortcomings in meeting the patient's needs. One can even say that a lot of this kind of 'pain' is the result of poor human contact and of a misunderstanding of the patient's situation. If this kind of patient would ask for euthanasia, it would be medically unjustified to comply with this request."[42]

Incompetent Patients and Advance Declarations.

Respect for the right of self determination by persons who are conscious and aware is easy to discuss and manage and there is virtually no disagreement on that issue. The plight of those who are mentally incompetent for any reason is not so easy either to discuss or to deal with in practice.

At present, in these latter conditions, close members of the family are regarded as surrogates in decision making, it being presumed that they are most likely to know what the patient would have wanted under the circumstances. While this works well enough as a rule, this is not always so. For example, the closest relative may not have been in contact with the patient for some time or there may be disagreement between family members about what should be done. To further complicate the issue, except for minors, the law confers no rights whatever on relatives to act in this role, not even spouses, though it is aware of what is usually done and accepts it as a practical solution. In the event of a legal dispute arising, however, the parties may be surprised to find that their position does not receive the support of the law which they had expected.

The matter of deciding on the most appropriate treatment in these circumstances involves close understanding with the family. This is best managed when the doctor has maintained a satisfactory relationship with them throughout the illness. Then, when a possibly contentious matter such as this needs to be decided in consultation, the parties already know and trust each other.

In recent years, and most notably in the US, advance declarations of various kinds have been proposed as offering an acceptable solution to decision making in this setting. These documents may be personally testified statements of intent that under certain circumstances, persons would want a particular course of action for themselves. They are usually called 'living wills', though such description may be merely one more example of terminology designed to distract, since they have nothing to do with living. They usually direct that when there is no hope of recovery and if the person is incompetent, no measures be adopted to prolong life and that efforts be restricted to providing comfort and relief.

The alternative kind of document, an 'enduring (or durable) power of attorney' directs that powers of decision making in such circumstances be vested in a nominated individual. Neither kind of document can contain instructions concerning an illegal act, and so, euthanasia cannot be included.

It can be seen that these devices are consistent with the rights of each person to determine appropriate treatment and to refuse unwanted treatment and that, when they are properly executed, they may be of great benefit in helping to direct decisions in otherwise difficult circumstances.

The legal status of these documents is far from clear, and varies from country to country, and even from state to state. Although the brief definition above makes them sound simple to draw up, they may be associated with complex interpretations. They have not been tested on many occasions and they must fulfill certain criteria in order to be valid. The Victorian parliamentary inquiry into Options for Dying with Dignity endorsed and recommended them[43], but the legislation which has now been enacted on the recommendation of that inquiry declined to consider the position of incompetent patients. It has been promised that this omission will soon be corrected. In the meantime, it would appear that in Victoria at least, such documents may not be legally valid.

The balance of opinion at present seems to be that, with certain reservations about their limitations, advance declarations may be quite helpful. Those who are still cautious are concerned about such matters as the conditions under which they may have been drawn up, the durability of the contained intention and doubt about their capacity in different circumstances to over-ride the doctor's perception of his duty to provide care to the best of his ability. Enough is now known about their potential for usefulness, however, to enable the law to engage in a closer consideration of their principles in order to try to overcome most of these difficulties, and hence encourage their wider, confident adoption.

Artificial Feeding of Incompetent Adults.

This may concern those who are dying or those who are

not. Regarding those who are terminally ill the method has not been a significant practical problem here. Prolongation of their life by these means is not commonly used for such patients unless there are unusual circumstances to justify it, and it is normally advised against as being inappropriate as a matter of principle. As in all such circumstances, good care requires that these and similar issues do not arise as an unaddressed possibility. If the family has been well communicated with, the question will have been anticipated, and even if that was not possible, the family will have been kept in close and understanding contact. Once a relationship of trust has been developed, all those measures which may be seen as inappropriate are more easily managed in co-operation.

The reason why a family may request this measure is on account of an erroneous idea that thirst will otherwise be a severe problem. While dying patients are often dehydrated to some degree, they rarely suffer thirst. Of course, if they do, this must be alleviated by keeping the mouth moist and by mouth care, and the same nursing care must routinely be given to incompetent or unconscious persons. Tube feeding and intravenous feeding are rarely needed for patient comfort, and instead, usually only succeed in prolonging dying, to the further distress of all parties.

In the US, with its more pronounced litigous environment, these practices were and perhaps still are, very frequent, as doctors were afraid not to do everything to preserve life, even those things which were thought to be inappropriate, for fear of legal action by some member of the family. The social consequences of this were often unsatisfactory for everyone. The courts have often been regarded in that country as the places where such issues are settled, although the courts themselves have tried to get the parties concerned to see that the proper way to deal with them is by honest personal transaction. The 'stand-off' between the parties is still perhaps too wide in many instances to encourage most individuals to risk the legal consequences. Over the past few years, there have been judgements in several US state jurisdictions to the effect that such tube feeding need not be routine, and that under certain conditions, it may be ceased, for example, when evidence can be produced that the patient would in all likelihood not have wanted it[44].

What happens in Australia in regard to the non-dying, those who are senile or stroke victims for instance, is variable and is determined by the judgement of those concerned. In these patients, tube feeding may have been started before the real prognosis had been determined and some time may have to elapse before the patient's real chances of recovery are clear. In most instances, it is preferable not to commence tube feeding, if that is thought to be the right course in the circumstances, rather than to have to discontinue it subsequently.

Illnesses Not Immediately Threatening Life.

It has been consistently claimed here that most of the physical distresses of the dying can be significantly alleviated as well as most of their emotional distresses. The same cannot be claimed for the groups of patients who have chronic, incurable illnesses which do not immediately threaten their lives, but will almost certainly eventually do so, but which may be responsible in the meantime for an unacceptably low quality of life for an indeterminate time. Such illnesses as multiple sclerosis, certain neuromuscular disorders, uncommon congenital defects and the results of injury such as quadriplegia are here included. Some of the frail elderly who are mentally competent fall into this category also.

While the will to live remains as strong in most of these people as in the rest of the population, despite objective evidence of disability which may confound the onlooker, some reach the stage where they wish for an end to their suffering. This may be due to physical causes but more often is due to an emotional exhaustion, brought on by the effort required to conduct their limited lives and the oppression of knowing that things can never get better. For some, they know they will inevitably get worse. Some are assailed by the quality of their dependence and an overwhelming sense of 'uselessness'. They know that their families may be drained by the effort of care, even when they do not complain, or that they themselves are a never ending and never rewarding focus of economic call on the community. The young may resent the injustice of a full life denied and the elderly may be depressed by the apparent futility of a life that will not end.

When their wish to die is not due to a passing fit of depression but is consistently and not unreasonably expressed, while every component of good care is already being provided, how should we respond? There is no answer which will suit all persons. Our total commitment may still not be enough, but we can't offer less.

Ultimately, we must acknowledge the limitations of any philosophy to lead to a satisfactory evaluation of our role in these circumstances. Either we accept our transcendent nature as a limitation on our ability to intervene in aspects of life which we do not understand, or we take power to ourselves, despite our ignorance. We have arrived at a mystery, whether we are prepared to admit it or not. We must await further enlightenment in these situations which, in many instances, are the outcomes of man's ingenuity, attributable to advances in social, medical and environmental factors. In another age, many such persons would already have died.

Referring to these people, the working party of the British Medical Association, which published its Euthanasia Report in 1988, said this: 'The subtle and dynamic factors surrounding disability and the wish to die make any drastic change in the law unwise for this group of patients'.[45] To be driven to kill in the name of humanity may be a temptation, but where, and how, will one then draw the line, once the motive of direct killing for social reasons has been accepted? Changing the general law to meet these hard cases would be the antithesis of what the law stands for, and lawyers acknowledge that.

Acquired Immuno Deficiency Syndrome. (A.I.D.S.)

The projected pandemic of death which is forecast from this cause in the near future necessitates some consideration of its place among other prominent causes of death from disease, and of whether this raises issues relevant to euthanasia. It is an illness unlike the present main life threatening diseases, in that it has its own special social settings and emotional components, it may produce different clinical syndromes, and it is transmissible.

If the general thesis of this book is to be sustained, namely that good care is the preferred solution to the problems of all the dying, then the care of these patients must be examined. Before proceeding to this, it can be observed that this is not a uniform challenge since several distinct patient groups are distinguishable as a result of the way in which AIDS has developed in the Western world. These are determined by the means by which the disease may be acquired. These groups, together with some of their important features, are:

— homosexual males. This is the largest group, consisting predominantly of young or middle aged men, often health conscious, articulate and from middle or upper socio-economic classes, having a large representation of writers and artists of many kinds, who are rejected to a significant degree by the rest of society and whose illness may be accompanied by powerful emotions. These include anger, resulting from their rejection, and guilt, perhaps associated with an awareness of the possibility, if not the certainty, of having already transmitted this fatal illness to another, perhaps loved, person.

— intravenous drug abusers. This may be the second largest group, now or in the future, consisting to a significant degree of persons from lower socio-economic classes, many or most of whom have personality disorders which predispose them to become social casualties of some kind.

— the infants of infected mothers, acquiring the disease in utero or at birth, or from drug abusing parents.

— those who have been accidentally infected by receiving a transfusion of contaminated blood. Their numbers are relatively low and this cause has now been effectively stopped by efficient screening methods at blood banks.

– the heterosexual partners of infected persons. The number of these is unknown in the West, but this route may be responsible for the greatest proportion of those infected in Africa.

Two questions have been given long and careful consideration in every part of the world:

Where and how is best care to be provided for persons dying from AIDS?

World wide experience with those dying of this illness has shown that their medical problems are best basically managed by use of the same principles as for other dying persons, with special provision for some of their unique aspects. These latter chiefly stem from: the relatively young age of most of the patients, problems arising from social alienation, some special clinical features and the possibility of concomitant drug abuse.

A problem not directly attributable to the illness itself has been the confused and, viewed from the standpoint of increased understanding, irrational response of the rest of society to the unexpected appearance of AIDS, not helped by the strident media. This has had particular impact on would-be carers, who have become fearful for their own health. Fortunately, this is now decreasing as a practical difficulty, as it becomes better known that the virus which causes the illness is really quite fragile and easily rendered harmless outside the human body, and that ordinary good nursing care protects the attendants from risk of infection.

At a practical level, it has been interesting to observe the ways in which the homosexual community itself has addressed the issue of care. They have often provided a loving supportive network to enable their dying members to remain as long as possible with them, where the victims have usually preferred to be, even when other and perhaps better accommodation has been available, assisted by trained community nurses, where possible. This community of men and women has thus been enabled to become unusually closely acquainted with dying and death, and by virtue of the calling of many of them, there has arisen a literature recording their experiences.

At a more organised level, when hospitalisation is required, it has been debated whether separate hospices should be established, to acknowledge the frequent preference of these patients for being with their own, or whether they would be better accommodated in a general hospice. The latter acknowledges that our caring resources are limited and must be used efficiently and also that, while community attitudes about AIDS need to be improved, this will be delayed by further segregation. Not surprisingly, each solution is being tried in different places, and both seem to work. A different proposal has been the 'small town' model and the 'large town' model, where a separate hospice may be provided where there is large number of cases, but not when the numbers are small. If there can be said to be a pattern, Australia seems to be opting for integration, rather than separation.

Only a brief reflection on the different categories of AIDS patients, listed above, is needed to be able to say that no particular type or place of care would be suitable or acceptable for all. Dying children and their parents will always need special kinds of care and adults will vary, depending on preference and physical state.

SOME AREAS OF DIFFICULTY

What then is the relevance of the foregoing, if any, to euthanasia?

To date, there has been little or no organised call for this practice for these dying persons, despite the fact that some of the ways in which this illness may develop may be as unpleasant as any elsewhere. There seem to be two likely reasons for this silence. First, the model of true care and support has been the one naturally adopted by the homosexual community to express their continuing feelings towards their dying companions, feelings perhaps more sharply focussed in their environment of relative isolation, and the same approach has been taken by the professionals who have treated them. These are the same motives of loving concern which prompt the call for better care of all dying persons, in other contexts.

Second, there may be a subtle awareness that pressure to provide euthanasia for most of these groups, already so patently disadvantaged in their living as well as their dying, would be the most inhumane insult which could be offered them. If any persons could be stigmatised as being both unwanted and a threat, it would be they. The challenge which persons suffering and dying from AIDS offers to contemporary society may be the most critical test which could be devised to highlight the central issues in the debate about euthanasia.

14

THE POSITION IN HOLLAND

The supporters of euthanasia frequently quote Holland as a country to be copied because voluntary euthanasia is actively practised there, but rarely is one told why it would be beneficial to do so. The benefit in being directly killed, even when one may be in distress, is not self evident. It is important, therefore, to be clear about what actually occurs in that country, because only then could one decide whether it would be advisable to follow the Dutch example. It also needs to be added that developments there seem to be taking place frequently and reports of current practices differ to some extent from one source to another. Some parts of the information below may soon be outdated.

So, one reads such things as: Dr X "hopes Australia will follow the lead of Holland where doctors have a policy of active euthanasia, and the patient's right to die is enshrined in the law." Most statements, like that one, prove to be a mixture of opinion and error.

Although it has been claimed that up to 10,000 instances of euthanasia per year occur in Holland, this figure includes so-called passive euthanasia[46], that is, the cessation of unwanted treatment. The number of instances of direct intentional killing is estimated as nearer to 1,000 per year, although over 80% of these are not reported as such. There appears to be a high level of community acceptance of the practice and although the factors which have led to that have been discussed many times, they are not agreed, nor is it clear that they would operate elsewhere. The Churches are divided on the matter, as are the doctors. The Royal Dutch Medical Association is supportive, having issued guidelines to members as to how they may circumspectly carry out euthanasia without falling foul of the law, though it does not regard as any form of euthanasia the practices described as passive euthanasia in chapter 4 of this book. Other doctors are appalled at the image of Holland as the 'killing capital' of Europe and a break-away medical group, the Netherlands League of Physicians, of 1,100 members, opposes euthanasia.

The Dutch literature on the subject contains the same elements as are to be found in other countries, namely the citing of examples of negligent care of the dying in order to justify euthanasia, with the implication that they represent the best that modern medicine can provide. There is also the same frequent use of euphemisms to soften or conceal the reality of what is being proposed. Common ways of referring to euthanasia are as 'careful medical treatment' or 'aid-in-dying'.

THE POSITION IN HOLLAND

An anaesthetist, Dr. Pieter Admiraal[42], speaks and writes freely and often of his role as a prominent provider of euthanasia. He plays no part in the care of the terminally ill, but merely responds to requests to kill, according to the guidelines listed below. He does not consider that his colleagues are proficient in palliative care, and this discipline has not yet been developed there. One commentator observed that there was no need for hospices. The methods of delivering euthanasia seem to be chiefly two, either a slow infusion of barbiturate to produce death in hours or an injection of barbiturate to produce rapid unconsciousness, followed by a muscle relaxant to produce respiratory arrest, which results in death within a few minutes. The former is preferred.

There is no formal legalisation of euthanasia in the Netherlands, either as direct killing or assisted suicide, and the present government has stated that it does not intend to change that. Three bills to attempt to effect change have not succeeded and two more are presently under consideration. Of these two, one would merely consolidate the present chaotic legal state of affairs, while the other would try to establish clear legal sanction for direct mercy killing.

Though euthanasia remains a criminal offence by statute, the real position now is bizarre, in that, provided euthanasia is carried out with certain precautions, which have not been formally accepted by the government, no prosecution will usually result.

In 1985, the State Commission on Euthanasia issued guidelines for medical practitioners, which have been adopted virtually unchanged by the Royal Dutch Medical Association[47], which now endorses euthanasia on demand, not only for competent adults, but also for minors, with or without their parents' consent. The approved indications include, in addition to terminal illness, conditions such as multiple sclerosis and paraplegia, which are not presently threatening life. It is currently being argued that, as well as voluntary euthanasia, involuntary .euthanasia should be available for conditions such as incurable psychiatric illnesses. Here, of course, the patient is incapable of consenting or dissenting.

The approved guidelines require that: the patient must be in an untenable position with no prospect of cure, the patient's request must be voluntary, rational and consistent, the patient must be fully informed, there must be no alternative treatment and a second doctor must be consulted.

No Provision to Supervise Guidelines.

There is no provision for any checking or supervision of these criteria. It is sufficient to report them as having been done, so there is not even any pretence that the legally recognised hazards to free choice, set out in chapter 6, are, at present, professionally determined or legally respected in Holland. Nor is there any requirement regarding the competence or, more importantly, the motivation of the certifying doctors. Thus, it is apparent that the protection which is due to all persons, whether they are patients or not, foreshadowed in British legal discussions and also set out in chapter 6, is denied the Dutch.

It is a simple and common matter to falsify the death certificate so that it appears that death was due to natural causes, and it is estimated that this occurs in the great majority of instances. Each case of reported euthanasia is examined by the Public Prosecutor, who will usually take little or no action, depending on circumstances. The penalty may be a fine, a prison term, which has been as short as one day, or most often a verdict of guilty, but without penalty. There is never a verdict of not guilty, when euthanasia has actually been reported. The maximum prison sentence has recently been reduced from 12½ years to 4½ years.

The statute law is now so disregarded and rendered powerless that involuntary euthanasia is already commonly performed. It has been reported that, as a result, elderly patients are afraid to be hospitalised and even to consult doctors.

How does this state of affairs compare with the way in which it is commonly represented in Australia? Dr. Kuhse is an open admirer of the Dutch methods, writing and speaking in support of them on every available occasion. In her article on 'Voluntary Euthanasia in the Netherlands' in 1987,[48] there was little mention of any of the important information above, no mention of extended indications or of involuntary euthanasia, no mention of the open disregard for the law or of the real situation being one of euthanasia on demand. In contravention of the evidence, it was erroneously stated there that the Dutch doctors take the question of consent 'very seriously indeed'.

Similary, in Dr. Kuhse's opinion poll of doctors in 1988, there was no mention of these same factors. In the light of the real situation, the questions put to the respondents were quite inadequate and misleading.

The extent to which the law is now captive in Holland was revealed by a recent reported case where nurses killed three comatose patients in an intensive care unit by injecting them with insulin and curare, without the knowledge or consent of the relatives[49]. They were charged with murder, but, although there was no doubt about the facts of the matter, they were discharged, because 'there was poor communication between the nurses and doctors over euthanasia policy'. Note that although they were charged with and had admitted murder, the stated failure of communication was over euthanasia policy, not murder policy. They were reprimanded and given a conditional jail sentence, conditional on their not being reported for the same offence within two years.

These were patients who could not give consent. According to Dutch law now, if nurses kill such persons, it is murder, but may not attract any penalty, but if doctors do the same, it is involuntary euthanasia and permissible. This is the point which has been reached in the country which we are being encouraged to emulate.

It seems hardly necessary to comment further, either on the current status of euthanasia in Holland or on the possible motives of those who misrepresent those practices. Readers must draw their own conclusions.

15

WHAT LIES AHEAD?

Most of this book's contents are centred on, and most obviously relevant to, Australia, but their implications are universal. It is critical then, when considering the future of the call for the legalisation of euthanasia in any country, to try to read the straws in the wind, wherever they may appear and wherever they may point. The debate has reached the stage where discussion is now global and continuous.

What may lie in the future for some countries may already be in prospect or in progress in others. Apart from Holland, it would appear that this is so in regard to proposals for euthanasia in the US, since more discussion about it, both public and private, seems to have occurred there. The movement to promote it is more organised, and the courts, which occupy a different role in some respects from their counterparts in other English speaking countries, have been more freely used to test the law in ways which would be unusual elsewhere. While events there may not necessarily constitute precedents for other places, they do need to be taken into account.

Future directions will be influenced by the ability to reason clearly while emotion is present, by an ability to be aware of and recognise disinformation and misinformation, because there is no shortage of either, and to be aware of the quality of humanity in various proposals, since all claim to be so motivated. This chapter will be devoted to defining some of these factors and the emphasis in many places will be on honesty, a leading casualty in the debate.

Self determination.

Most public discussion is directed toward voluntary euthanasia, and most of its advocates present it as an example, perhaps the ultimate example, of self determination. Narrowly defined, self determination may be intended to mean that an individual may determine what happens or does not happen to himself. Since an individual may wish for many impossible things, its realisation, on that definition alone, is also impossible. More broadly and more realistically, it may mean that the individual wishes to take full responsibility for his actions and his destiny.

By that criterion, the proposal that one is anxious to take decisions but not to act upon them personally, even when it is quite possible to do so, which is what is being advocated in most instances of voluntary euthanasia, is not consistent with a claim of self determination. This principle would require that suicide was the autonomous response to an individual's determination that death was his preferred solution to his personal problem, and that suicide should be advocated for those who were of this mind and who were physically able to perform it.

Clearly, this would not be a popular proposal. Some would say that by the time they wanted to die, they would be physically unable to carry it out or they would have no means to do so. All persons who wished to be self reliant could prepare themselves for such an eventuality while they were in good health. Some would say it is an inhuman proposition, considering the possible circumstances of the person in extremis who may be asking for euthanasia, and that can be conceded. Whatever the practicalities of the matter, it is in no instance an example of the principle of self determination. It should be obvious that I am not advocating suicide for such persons.

Derek Humphry, co-founder of the Hemlock Society, the largest society in the US for the promotion of euthanasia, wrote in 1984 "pain is by no means the only reason, if at all, why people contemplate self-deliverance, with or without assistance. Control and choice of when, where, and how, plus personal dignity and a wish to avoid distress, physical and emotional, during the dying process are the key considerations."[50] This is a plea for euthanasia on demand, on the patient's terms. But having decided on the control and choice of when, where and how, it is assumed that the person, even when capable of carrying out the action, will now turn to another and say in effect "I have decided what I want, but I want you to carry it out for me." Whatever may be said of that, it is a mockery of a genuine human principle.

Why is it felt necessary to cloak a pedestrian proposal in the guise of principle, if not because it has so little otherwise to recommend it genuinely?

Is self determination to be the prerogative of patients only? It is often claimed that those doctors who object to euthanasia would be under no obligation to take part in any legalised scheme. Already, in Holland, there is an expectation that when a doctor is asked for euthanasia, if he is unwilling to carry it out personally, it will be his responsibility to refer the patient to another doctor who will oblige. The probable reason why he would refuse would be on conscientious grounds, or it may be that the decision was in conflict with his reading of his valid duty of care, in the circumstances. In either case, in referring the patient on, he must act against his conscience, if conscience means anything at all. Presumably, he may not self determine.

Euthanasia on demand.

Discussion of voluntary euthanasia most often proceeds on the understanding that it is being sought for those who have unrelievable distress, usually physical, and usually associated with terminal illness. That is the context in which most attempts at law reform anywhere to date have been framed. When caution is sounded by any person, on the ground that such a law may subsequently be widened to include other applications, deprecatory accusations of Nazi scaremongering are to be expected. The evidence is that such warnings are only too likely to be fulfilled.

There should be no doubt whatever that eventual extension to further applications is proposed, and in Holland, they are currently in operation. To suppose that these extensions would be able to be resisted is to ignore the historical precedents.

WHAT LIES AHEAD?

Again, the literature of Hemlock and comparable societies, not for general circulation, provides the clue to their contemporary thinking. In addition to claiming to represent the terminally ill, Hemlock includes the 'seriously incurably physically ill', among whom their recent writings would include those with Alzheimer's Disease and even osteoporosis.[51] Humphry advocates the 'right' of quadriplegics to euthanasia.[52] How much more broadly could the following reference to euthanasia be written: "When should it be done? We are only here once (or so I believe) and it is folly to leave it too long. Decide what is (sic) the criteria for an acceptable quality of life for you."

As to current realities, the Rotterdam Criminal Court in 1981 decided that an applicant for euthanasia need not be terminally ill, paraplegics may be included.[53] The Dutch medical representatives at the World Voluntary Euthanasia Conference in 1980 claimed that euthanasia was available virtually 'on demand' in their country. Hemlock commented that this was 'advanced'.[54]

Any person who doubts the likelihood that this extension would follow the legalisation of euthanasia in any place, is invited to consider the world wide phenomenon of the existing availability of abortion in those countries where it is legal, and compare it with the hypocrisy of the pre-legal claims. For example, in the 1970s in the US, the main indications were set out as rape, incest or danger to the mother's health. In 1982, 1.5 million abortions were being performed annually in that country, as many as 99% of which were for economic reasons or convenience.[55] The position is not different in kind in Australia, UK or New Zealand.

Reference to the evolution of euthanasia in Nazi Germany draws the response that such comment is emotional, insulting and inappropriate. Who would want to emulate those monsters? Precisely the same arguments are being advanced to support euthanasia to-day as were advanced there, as will be elaborated in the later section on the argument for euthanasia, based on cost.

Involuntary euthanasia.

Involuntary euthanasia is rarely advocated openly except for the killing of disabled newborn infants, though the internal pro-euthanasia literature contains regular reference to its various forms. It has already been mentioned that involuntary euthanasia is argued for and, in fact, practised presently in Holland. One such report described it as 'rampant', in defiance of the law.[56]

The legal criteria, which would have to be satisfied in order to be sure that consent to being killed was freely and competently given, were listed in chapter 6. There, it was also mentioned that one of the reasons why euthanasia has not been legalised thus far has been the inability of the law to guarantee such freedoms.

In the case of persons who are frankly mentally incompetent, there are at present no ways of satisfactorily resolving the issue of consent to or dissent from treatment, which are considered to guarantee their best interests. Proxies, either a family member or another nominated substitute, will use their own standards to do this, hopefully to the best of their ability. Whose interests will they represent, their own or the patient's? Even with the best will, when the continued life of the person represents a conflict of interests or a burden on somebody, perhaps not the proxy, not even the proxy may be able to say that the decision was objective, and an outsider certainly could not.

The different forms of involuntary euthanasia are promoted by the same persons who advocate voluntary euthanasia. But now a surprising shift in emphasis occurs. Whereas voluntary euthanasia is described as resting on the principle of self determination, (erroneously, as noted above), the same element is lacking from the arguments for involuntary euthanasia, to the extent that it is not even mentioned. The justification for involuntary euthanasia is now stated to be the welfare of other parties, such as the family or society at large, measured in terms of threat to emotional stability or actual money cost.

It is certain that quality of life has no direct relationship to bodily integrity. The fittest are not per se the happiest, and the disabled are just as keen on being alive as any other group. What then has become of the claimed important principle of self determination to justify euthanasia if it can be so easily jettisoned for expedient reasons? If it is valid at all, it should be presumed to be strongly operative for all, and for those who cannot express their intention, it should logically be the more strongly presumed and promoted. Instead, we find that, for them, quite other standards are adopted, whereby only the interests of other parties are admitted for consideration. That approach is lacking in consistency and honesty.

When we come to the killing of disabled infants, the position is most unsatisfactory. In the previous discussion on this topic, it was mentioned that this practice occurs presently to an unknown extent, though some have said it is widespread, and that the justification for it rests on arguably untenable grounds at best and on illegal grounds at all times. The commonest medical conditions for which it is proposed are spina bifida and Down syndrome. Except for a minority of cases, it cannot be known at birth what quality of life the infant may have in later life, with or without surgery.

In one series of almost one thousand unselected cases of spina bifida,[57] by school age, 75% of the children had normal intelligence, more than 80% were ambulatory, almost 90% were continent, 99% of the parents were satisfied with the outcome and the parental divorce rate was one fifth of the national average. By contrast, another group reported that 48% of such babies were denied nourishment, for reasons that the family "felt vigorous, long term care of this baby would have added undue stress to their family unit." This judgement does not respect any interpretation of presumed self determination, nor the child's best interests.

The situation with regard to Down syndrome is worse. Such children are known to be generally affectionate and happy, have varying degrees of retardation, though usually mild, and have never been known to commit suicide. In one hospital series,[58] 22% of doctors favoured witholding nutrition from such infants, even though they had no other complications. They were to be killed merely because they had been born with that defect.

The rationale for this is the anticipated effects on the family's economics, the welfare of other children or the parents' capacity to cope. These reasons are social, and are distorted so as to deny natural justice to the infant. They go further than a declaration that some lives are not worth living, and extend to an assumption of power to deny life to some of those whose lives are demonstrably worth living.

That is homicide 'with malice aforethought.'

The present Surgeon General of the US, Dr. C Everett Koop, commented on this situation thus: "semantics have made infanticide palatable by never referring to the practice by that word, but by using such euphemisms as 'selection'. 'Starving a child to death' becomes 'allowing him to die'. It is all illegal but the law has turned its back. The day will come when the argument will be as it was for abortion, 'Let's legalise what is already happening.' Then, what is legal is right."[59]

It is quite logical to suppose, therefore, that if voluntary euthanasia were to be made legal, the call for its extension to those who are unable to consent would be only a matter of time.

Economics.

When this matter was treated earlier, it was projected that economic factors may become a dominant issue in the future. In some places, they are already so. Efforts at cost containment can create serious conflicts of interest for vulnerable groups who may feel themselves, correctly or not, the targets for unwelcome action. The arguments can also be brought to the point where the only 'reasonable' decision is in favour of compliance. This is easy to do when the subjects are in no position to speak for themselves, either literally or metaphorically.

In California, brochures directed to parents regarding ante-natal genetic screening programs stress the savings to be made by the state by not having spina bifida and Down syndrome infants survive.[60]

The Executive Director of the American Euthanasia

Foundation suggested to the government that some two billion dollars could be saved annually and overcrowding could be eliminated by distributing living wills to Veterans Administration hospital patients, whereby 'no hope veterans' could be allowed to die.[61] A former head of the Health Care Financing Administration in the US pointed out that a national system of living wills could have saved that country $1.2 billion in 1978.[62]

Setting aside the moral dimensions of these proposals, these sums may appear large, but they become miniscule when compared with annual private spending on such items as pornography, recreation, illegal drugs, pets, jewellery and other personal possessions. What is staggering is not the size of these amounts but that the proposals are being made publicly, while there is not any real economic necessity to do so, in a country which is still one of the richest in the world. They reflect a consumeristic, egocentric value system and they are in direct line with the economic arguments advanced in Germany in the 1930s.

Is Philosophy Always Helpful?

A prominent feature of the discussions on euthanasia in recent years has been the frequent contributions from philosophers. Philosophy is devoted to the study of the principles of human conduct. Since its determinations cannot be subjected to agreed, objective testing, its methods and conclusions must be judged by the quality of the evidence or argument on which they rest.

In opening the 18th. World Congress of Philosophy in Great Britain in 1988, its organiser, Professor Allen Phillips Griffiths, said "You study it because you're absolutely fascinated by it, but the fact is, philosophy is quite useless."[63] Not many of his colleagues, and not many other people, would be fully in agreement with him on that opinion, but it does address an important concept, namely that philosophy does not and cannot go to the detail of the practical consequences which may flow from its thinking. To attempt to do this is to exceed its valid limits. Of course, philosophers are as entitled to their opinions on any subject as any other person, but these opinions, like those of any other person, are worth no more than the gounds on which they stand.

As earlier stated, the common philosophy in support of euthanasia, in one or other of its forms, is utilitarianism. In 'Utilitarianism, For and Against' published in 1973,[9] co-authored by Bernard Williams, when Provost of King's College, Cambridge, that author drew conclusions about it which are strongly critical. The full text should be consulted by interested readers for greater detail, but the following comments represent some of his views.

He concluded that, although it is an important system, it is, among other things, cocksure, unrestrainedly arbitrary, primitive in its determination of equity, simple minded in its dealing with complex human conditions (there cannot be many more complex human conditions than those which surround dying) and at some points, rests on illusion. Classic Benthamism he sees as egoistic. That which is arbitrary is 'derived from mere opinion, capricious.'[64] If true, that can hardly be accepted as a sound basis on which to construct a set of principles to determine the taking of innocent human life.

Some Australian utilitarian philosophers, in dealing with euthanasia, do step beyond philosophical debate and into the market place. In relation to medical matters, they display ignorance of many of the central issues, both in questions of care and the vital aspects of human interchange in the professional relationships with the sick. Being themselves professionals of another kind, they should appreciate the limits of their competence. The practical components of good care of the dying and the disabled arise from a deep understanding of what these patients need and genuinely want, based on extensive experience. Neither the seriously ill, nor the society of which they are part, will be helped by intellectual judgements, considered in isolation from the human realities of their condition.

It is probably more important to note that, although these commentators are aware of the steps needed to effect change to produce improved care of all dying patients, they remain silent and uncommitted to the wider introduction of these changes, but continue as vocal proponents of socially regressive policies. Worse, their views in certain areas have, as their primary effect, the facilitation of the destruction of some of the most dependent members of the community. This may be a uniquely low point for any philosophical principle which claims respectability, namely that its application has no beneficial primary social outcomes, whatever.

Law Reform.

Two recent overseas initiatives with future implications merit comment.
i. Attempts to Change the Law by Side-Stepping the Parliament.
   In the US, in the state of California and in some other

states also, it is permissible to include a question regarding a proposed law on a state ballot paper, if sufficient signatures have been obtained beforehand to support such a move. If the question then gains enough votes, the Act referred to in the question becomes the law. By this means, the normal judicial processes of law making by parliamentary debate, with all their inbuilt protective checks, can be by-passed, and public opinion alone, informed or otherwise, can determine the law.

This device was tried early in 1988 by the radical leadership of some of the pro-euthanasia groups in California, but without success. 'Americans Against Human Suffering' and The Hemlock Society, led by Derek Humphry, failed to find a parliamentarian who would sponsor their proposed legislation, to be called The Humane and Dignified Death Act, 1988, in the State Assembly. So they then sought enough signatures from the public to enable a question about the proposed law to be included on the ballot paper for the State elections which were soon to be held, as outlined above, but also failed to achieve that. They attributed their lack of success to lack of time and organisation, and have given notice that they intend to repeat the exercise in the permitted time, that is, after a lapse of two years, in California and perhaps also in Oregon, Washington and Florida.

The Speaker of the Assembly in California, who is said to favour legalised euthanasia, has criticised these moves, on the ground that, in his view, the parliamentary process is the safe and proper way to achieve change, in order that the matter can be debated in an open and informed way.

If the proposed change had genuine public support, there would be no reason to circumvent the normal processes of law making, established as the most effective means to afford protection for all citizens. The only reasons to choose the devious path would be an awareness that the proposal could not withstand the informed and open scrutiny it would necessarily encounter in the parliament or a desire to achieve change at any cost. Not even Hemlock was surprised that it could not find a member of the Assembly to sponsor the Bill. If such manoeuvres succeed in the future, it will be necessary for other countries with different legal systems to be fully aware of the methods used to bring about that change and to decide carefully whether such might be regarded as a suitable legal precedent or just a dodge, in line with so much of the other subterfuge and double talk associated with this subject.

ii. A New Enunciation of an Old Right.

Pro-euthanasia groups from different countries have banded together to form the World Federation of Right-To-Die Societies. At the 7th. Biennial Conference of that Federation in San Francisco in April 1988, Helga Kuhse presented the draft of a submission which she had been asked to prepare, for the consideration of its constituent societies. Some of these national bodies have only a few hundred members and some support only the practices incorrrectly labelled as passive euthanasia, and previously discussed. The draft is intended as a submission to be forwarded to the Human Rights Commission of the United Nations, recommending the incorporation of a statement of a 'right to die with dignity' as an appendix to the Charter of Human Rights, 1948.[65]

While a right to die with dignity is an unexceptionable concept, the record of the groups taking these steps, on their past interpretations of rights, makes it necessary to examine the proposition carefully. It is being claimed that, since death may now be postponed for some patients because of advanced medical technology, it is no longer a natural event and has become a matter of human choice. That being the case, it is argued it should be the patient who will choose.

All that has changed in reality in recent years is the determination of the timing, not the fact, of death. The choice of that timing, in law and in practice, resides with the patient in his or her right to refuse treatment which is unwanted, so nothing has altered with regard to his or her autonomy. The advances of modern medicine have no bearing on the issue of what constitutes a fundamental human right, and certainly have not been responsible for the creation of a new right which did not previously exist, that is, the right to be killed. If any persons still wish to claim that there is a right to be killed, and especially if they are disguising their real intentions by hiding them behind bland but misleading terms, they will still need to argue their case, not simply assert it or imply it.

Several of the clauses of the draft would be open to widely differing interpretations. For example, clause 3 reads, "The dying person's wishes concerning death and the dying processes must be respected and not restricted. Decisions against the will of the patient, either on the part of the state, physicians or other institutions or persons, are not in accordance with human rights". Without qualification, that is a most inadequate and inaccurate statement of rights. A literal interpretation of the last section would be that a person has a right to whatever he asks for. It is certain that the proposers would intend it to mean that if a person asked to be killed, his wish must be complied with. How would they interpret that right if the patient asked instead to be sent, together with all his family, at public expense, to the other side of the world for further treatment? If he must have the one without question, must he not also have the other?

The draft document's compiler, Dr Kuhse, usually makes a distinct point of not discussing the concept of rights at all, and at present does nothing in practice to support the existing legitimate right of all dying patients, in Australia and elsewhere, to death with dignity. Can it then be supposed she will make such use of the proposal as will enhance the human condition of dying persons generally? How may it be expected that she will interpret her phrase in clause 1, "the right to painless dying", when she presently aligns herself with Right To Die organisations which instead propose the right to be killed, and when she herself uses "assistance in dying" to mean "killing"?

An objectionable and unnecessary phrase is included in clause 5 where, after referring to the valid right of a person to refuse any religious ministrations, it goes on to add that the dying "must not be subjected to religious observances that have not been specifically requested." That is gratuitously insulting to the men and women who, traditionally through the ages and ante-dating the involvement of the state in health care by several centuries, have been and still are among those who provide the highest standards of care for the sick, especially the dying. Unless it can be shown that there is at present substantial forcing of religious observance on those who do not wish it, the phrase merely indicates a further instance of lack of true awareness of current practices and an irrelevant, antagonistic attitude of the author.

WHAT LIES AHEAD?

This projected appeal to the Human Rights Commission of the United Nations stands in stark contrast with its author's current sweeping disregard for another of that body's declarations – The Declaration of the Rights of the Child, particularly as it relates to the disabled. This declaration has already been quoted as defining the handicapped child's right to "the special treatment, education and care required by his particular condition". These are the very children whom her University department has arbitrarily redefined as non-persons, and then declared them to be less entitled to their right to life than an adult animal. In light of that observation, an approach to the United Nations in the proposed terms could only be seen as an impudent and cynical exercise.

Obtaining a declaration of a right to die with dignity in the terms of her proposal would be a prelude to renewed and, if based on such document, spurious attempts at reform of the domestic law to enable euthanasia. A recent newspaper editorial made some simple, straightforward comment on the reality of the situation: "Some advocates of euthanasia want mercy killing to be made legal. But as well as provoking moral outrage and overturning a basic rule of society, this course would be dangerous. It could very easily lead to the death of people who are not so much sick as troublesome to others. And it could see terrible pressures being exerted on doctors by the families of the troublesome."[66] Since patients already have the legitimate right to death with dignity, perhaps what we really need to articulate is the right and the responsibility of doctors to treat with dignity, free from unwarranted pressures.

EUTHANASIA

More Opinion Polls?

Reference has already been made to the fallibility of polls to reflect informed opinion, particularly on complex subjects, though it should not surprise that people try to confuse by capitalising on such data. It is to be more strongly regretted when professional ethicists also engage in the use of euphemisms and the drawing of unwarranted conclusions from data.

In their poll of doctors' attitudes to euthanasia, Kuhse and Singer have done that. They engage in special pleading to the extent of claiming that the current policies of the Australian Medical Association on euthanasia must be questioned, though they are in accord with those of virtually every other national medical association in the world, on the basis of replies to this effect from only 24% of those polled. When considering the momentous decision to take innocent human life, it is worse. Now, when only 28% of those polled agreed that "it is sometimes right for a doctor to take active steps to bring about the death of the patient", and appealing to the flawed Morgan poll (page 60) for support, it was claimed that this constituted "a strong case for changing the law" to permit euthanasia.

When the failed Humane and Dignified Death Act, mentioned above, was being proposed in California, the California Medical Association, representing the majority of the doctors of that state, opposed it and reaffirmed that organisation's ethical opposition to euthanasia. A group, titled the San Francisco Medical Society, then conducted a poll of 1,743 doctors with the following questions: 1. "Do you feel that patients should have the option of requesting active euthanasia when faced with incurable terminal illness?" and

2. "If you feel that legalisation of active voluntary euthanasia would be appropriate, do you think that physicians should be the ones to carry out such requests?" 70% of respondents answered in the affirmative to the first and 54% to the second question.

With characteristic disregard for the truth, these results have been quoted to demonstrate high levels of support for the practices mentioned. When it is realised, however, that only 38% of those polled replied, the only accurate interpretation to be placed on the results is that it is known that 26% of those polled supported the first question and 20% the second. Any other interpretation is speculation only.

No doubt, opinion polls will be conducted in the future to try to determine the attitudes of various groups about euthanasia. It must not be forgotten that, at best, they represent opinions only, most often opinions not based on adequate information or understanding, and that, even when well carried out, these polls contribute nothing whatever to the determination of the correctness of an ethical issue.

It is disappointing and sad for me to find repeated examples of deviousness, selectivity and insincerity in the writings of the more vocal supporters of euthanasia. I suspect they do not mirror the true feelings of most of those who genuinely but misguidedly support euthanasia, and I know, from personal experience, they do not reflect the true feelings of most of society, including those without any religious affiliation, formal or otherwise. When falsity is necessary to make a case, the case is weak, and those who engage in falsity further devalue it and themselves.

In the sections above, there is evidence of extreme positions, a basic lack of respect for human life, in some instances well intentioned but short-sighted proposals, and confusion. These cannot be expected to change in future discussions, so it will be important to be able to recognise them and to be able to take them into account when assessing the worth of future comments. Dr. Leo Alexander, US medical consultant to the Nuremberg trials, described in 1949 the enormity of the consequences of permissive attitudes towards the capricious taking of some lives, as revealed at those trials.[8] Almost forty years later, in 1984, he said of similar practices in the US, "It is much like Germany in the twenties and thirties. The barriers against killing are coming down."[67]

16

CONCLUSION

A proposal to amend the law to allow the taking of innocent human life, under certain conditions, can be seen as such an enormous departure from traditional and existing moral and legal principles, and could have such extensive and unpredictable consequences, that it demands the greatest possible amount of careful consideration. It is evident that a bad law in this regard would be tragic, and that such tragedies would be irreversible. There is no precedent for such a law in any major legal code, despite the fact that reviews to examine the possibility of law reform have been carried out on numerous occasions.

The central challenge posed to individuals by a proposal for euthanasia is to formulate a sound ethical response on which practical detail may be grafted. If individuals are not able to do this, the next best response is to try to weigh possible advantages and disadvantages, both for persons and society. Either or both of these processes entail taking note of a large number of factors, involving an understanding of some of the workings of complex disciplines. There is need to raise the level of debate to take these complexities into account, because many of them are currently merely ignored.

By failing to address certain of the chief elements, the credibility of those who argue for euthanasia is diminished. Specifically, they fail to acknowledge that law reform, in any form which has so far been proposed, may have such undesirable consequences that the outcome may be worse than the existing problems, and they fail to offer adequate support for the cause of better care for all the dying, by which the need to ask for euthanasia may be greatly reduced or abolished.

It is a bitter paradox that euthanasia is being promoted, primarily because of poor medical care, at a time when we know better than ever before, how to care well for the dying. The medical profession has in its hands the best social answer to the call for euthanasia. It is at once the partial cause of the problem and the best hope for the effective remedy.

The advocates of euthanasia must also be aware of this paradox and must bear their share of the responsibility for a positive, life respecting solution. By any criterion, it must be ethically superior to attend to the elimination of human distress before the elimination of the human in distress. I suggest that, in any other sphere of human activity, if it were proposed that people in distress should be killed in preference to applying the known and proven remedies for

CONCLUSION

the relief of that distress, the proposal would be seen as grotesque and anti-human, and would be universally condemned. If any persons believe that the necessary remedies to provide this relief are not yet presently available on a sufficiently wide scale, they each have an equal responsibility to work to change that.

The need to reform medical education to prepare doctors to care well for the dying is greater than, and more urgent than, the need for law reform.

The dying, possibly the most vulnerable group of the sick, need uniformly high standards of care, and they need all the protection the law can provide to guarantee that their genuine rights are always protected. One of the measures of a civilised society is the degree to which it protects its weakest members.

Based on the evidence which has been presented in this book, I conclude that the case for euthanasia:
- rests on premises which do not respect life
- rests ethically on unsupported assertion
- is commonly presented in misleading terms
- is not supported by medical codes of ethics
- is not supported by legal analysis
- is at odds with current best medical strategies of care
- is at odds with patients' best interests and
- is at odds with society's best interests.

REFERENCES

1. Saunders C M ed. 1979. The Management of Terminal Disease; Arnold.
2. Twycross R and Lack S. 1984. Therapeutics in Terminal Cancer; Pitman.
3. Stedeford A. 1984. Facing Death; Heinemann. Chap 12.
4. Lichter I. 1987. Communication in Cancer Care; Churchill Livingstone. p. 178.
5. Social Development Committee. Report upon the Inquiry into Options for Dying with Dignity. Parliament of Victoria. April 1987.
6. Binding K and Hoche A. 1920. Permission to Destroy a Life Not Worth Living; Its Extent and Form, Reviewed in The Right of Putting Incurable Patients Out of The Way. 1920. J. Am. Med. Assn 75:1283.
7. Wertham F. 1973. A Sign for Cain; An Exploration of Human Violence.
8. Alexander L. 1949. Medical Science under Dictatorship; New Eng. J. Med. 241:39 et seq.
9. Smart JJ and Williams B. 1973. Utilitarianism, For and Against. Cambridge University Press.
10. Downing AB and Smoker B eds. 1986. Voluntary Euthanasia; Peter Owen. p. 97.
11. Declaration of Euthanasia. 1987. Lancet; 1:1505.
12. The Euthanasia Report. Brit. Med. Assn. London, BMA, 1988.
13. Singer P. 1979. Practical Ethics, Cambridge University Press. p. 97.

14. Bentham J. Anarchical Fallacies. Reprinted in: Melden A I, ed. Human Rights, 1970. Belmont; Wadsworth, p. 32.
15. Natural Death Act, 1983. South Australia.
16. Medical Treatment Act, 1988. Victoria.
17. sup. note 10. p.27.
18. International Covenant on Civil and Political Rights. Proclaimed by the General Assembly, U.N. on 16. 12. 1966. Resolution 2200 (a) (xxi). Australia in common with its western counterparts, UK, USA, NZ, Canada is a signatory.
19. Declaration of the Rights of the Child. Proclaimed by the General Assembly, U.N. on 20.11.1959. Resolution 1386 (xiv).
20. Declaration of the Rights of Mentally Retarded Persons. Proclaimed by the General Assembly, U.N. on 20.12.1971. Resolution 2856 (xxvi).
21. Declaration of the Rights of the Disabled. Proclaimed by the General Assembly, U.N. on 9.12.1975. Resolution 34447 (xxx).
22. Law of Murder, Melbourne; Law Reform Commissioner, Report 1, August 1974 p.225.
23. sup. note 5, Recommendation 1, page v.
24. Criminal Law Revision Committee, Working paper on Offences Against the Person, HMSO, 1976.
25. Euthanasia, Aiding Suicide and Cessation of Treatment. Law Reform Commission of Canada. Report 20, 1983.
26. Humphry D. Mrs. Bouvia's Sad Mistakes are Lessons. 1984. Hemlock Q. 1 p. 14.
27. Lamerton R. 1980. Care of the Dying. Pelican Press. p. 146.
28. sup. note 10. Gillon R quoted at p. 210.
29. Singer P and Wells D. 1984. The Reproduction Revolution. Oxford University Press. p. 203.
30. sup. note 13. p. 131.
31. sup. note 13. p. 138.
32. sup. note 13. p. 131.
33. Concise Oxford Dictionary.
34. Legal and Ethical Aspects of the Management of the Newborn with Severe Disabilities. Occasional Paper No 10 of the Australian Human Rights Commission. August 1985.
35. Brahams D. Severely handicapped babies and the law, 1986. Lancet, April 28, p. 984.
36. Majority favour mercy killing. Morgan Research Centre Poll. May, 1986.
37. sup. note 5. p. 155.
38. Kuhse H and Singer P. Doctors' practices and attitudes regarding voluntary euthanasia. Med. J. Aust. 1988 148:623-626.
39. Williams G. 1958. The Sanctity of Life and the Criminal Law. p. 311-312.
40. Wanzer SH Adelstein SL et al. The physician's responsibility toward

REFERENCES

hopelessly ill patients. New Eng J Med. 1984. 310:955-959.

41. Higgs R. Not the last word on euthanasia. 1988. Brit. Med. J. 296:1348.
42. sup. note 10. p. 186.
43. sup. note 5. Recommendation 21 page viii.
44. Curran WJ. 1985. Defining Appropriate Care: Providing Nutrients and Hydration for the Dying. New Eng J Med. 313:940-942.
45. Euthanasia: conclusions of a BMA working party set up to review the association's guidance on euthanasia. 1988. Brit. Med. J. 296:1377.
46. Weekend Australian. July 4, 1987.
47. Borst-Eilers E. 1987. Letter, Brit. Med. J. 295:1564.
48. Kuhse H. Voluntary euthanasia in the Netherlands. Med. J. Aust. 1987. 147:394-396.
49. News Exchange of the World Federation of Doctors who Respect Life. Belgium, April, 1988. p. 34.
50. Humphry D. Let Me Die Before I Wake. 1984. p. 76.
51. Humphry D and Wickett A. The Right to Die: Understanding Euthanasia 1986. p. 313.
52. Humphry D. The Suicide Shambles, book review. 1982. Hemlock Q. 3. p.7.
53. Van Till. Dutch Doctors Get Guidelines. 1984. Hemlock Q. 1. p. 17.
54. Note, World Conference. 1980. Hemlock Q. 1 p.1.
55. US Senate Committee on the Judiciary, Human Life Federalism Amendment, S. Rep. No. 465, 1982, 97th Congress, 2nd. Sess, 50 n. 256.
56. Parachini. The Netherlands debates the legal limits of euthanasia, Los Angeles Times, July 5, 1987.
57. McLone, Dias, Kaplan and Sommers. 1985. Concepts in the management of Spina Bifida, in Concepts Pediatric Neurosurgery. pp. 97-106.
58. Note, Treating the defective newborn: A survey of physicians attitudes. 1976. Hastings Centre Rep. p. 2.
59. Koop CE. Ethical and surgical considerations in the care of the newborn with congenital abnormalities, in Infanticide and the Handicapped Newborn; Horan and Delahoyde eds. 1982. pp. 89-106.
60. California State Department of Health Services, Fiscal Analysis of Impact of Maternal Serum Screening to Detect Neural Tube Defects (projection for fiscal year 1985-1986).
61. Death with Dignity: An Inquiry into Related Public Issues: Hearings Before the Special Committee on Ageing. US Senate, 92nd. Congress, 1972. 2nd. Sess. p. 30.
62. Derzon R. Memorandum on Additional Cost Saving Initiatives, June 4, 1977.
63. Sydney Morning Herald, August 25, 1988.
64. Concise Oxford Dictionary.
65. Report No. 61, Voluntary Euthanasia Society of Victoria. August 1988.

EUTHANASIA

66. Editorial, The Newcastle Herald, NSW. September 14, 1988.
67. Derr, The Real Brophy Issue. Boston Globe, November 18, 1985.

INDEX

Abortion 47, 115

Acquired Immuno Deficiency Syndrome (AIDS) 99

Active euthanasia 21

Admiraal, Dr P. 92, 107

Advance declarations 42, 94

Alexander, Dr L. 130

Allowing to die 28, 30

Alzheimer's Disease 115

Animal life, value of 30, 52, 53, 127

Appropriate medical treatment 3, 80, 81, 94, 96

Arbitrariness 40, 52, 54, 121, 127

Artificial feeding 95

Assertion 27, 29, 31, 33, 37, 52, 125, 133

Autonomy 13, 14, 29, 55, 70, 80, 93, 94, 112, 113, 114, 125

Bentham, J. 26, 31, 121

Binding, K. 19

BMA Working Party on Euthanasia 99

British Medical Association 28

California Medical Association 128

Canada, Law Reform Commission 45

Cancer 7, 8, 15, 18, 63, 80, 86

Christian views 3, 31, 34, 36

Common law 13, 33, 41

Communication 10, 12, 78, 94, 96

Compassion 5, 20, 41, 46, 57

Competence, mental 22, 108

Coping skills 91

Costs of medical care 20, 67, 68, 119

Criminal Law Revision Committee 45

Deception 11, 12

Denial 10, 91

Disabled persons 5, 40, 41, 51, 56, 67, 115, 116, 117, 122

Down Syndrome 55, 118

Duties 33, 34

Education, medical 44, 74, 77, 79, 81, 89, 133

Emotional aspects of euthanasia 2, 5, 59, 112

Emotional distress 8, 9, 17, 23, 46, 64, 90, 97, 98

Emotional support 10, 11, 29, 78, 82

Empathy 11, 74

Ethics 1, 3, 23, 27, 42, 43, 57, 74, 131, 133

Eugenics 55, 69

Euphemisms 3, 30, 55, 61, 106

  for killing:

  aid in dying 106

  allowing to die 28, 30, 119

  assistance in dying 61, 126

  benign neglect 57

  careful medical treatment 106

  helping not to survive 55

  selection 119

Euthanasia on demand 107, 113, 114

Family 4, 10, 12, 16, 56, 57, 64, 91, 93, 96, 116, 118

Germany 19, 115, 130

Gillon, Dr R. 47

Griffiths, Prof A. 120

Hemlock Society 113, 115, 123, 124

Heroin 88

Hitler, A. 20

Hoche, A. 19

Holland 47, 105 et seq., 114, 115, 116

Homicide 21, 22, 39, 40, 42

Honesty 3, 4, 8, 33, 112, 117, 129

Hospice (see also palliative care) 17, 102

Human life, value of 1, 4, 25, 30, 35, 52, 53

Human Rights Commission, Australia 54

Human Rights Commission, United Nations 124

Humphry, D. 113, 115, 123

Incompetence, mental 20, 22, 40, 67, 93 et seq., 95, 116

Infants, see Newborn

Inquiry into Options for Dying with Dignity 13, 23, 44, 60, 78, 95

International Covenant on Civil and Political Rights 40

INDEX

Involuntary (non
  voluntary) euthanasia
  22, 51,116

Judeo-Christian ethic 52

Killing 3, 21, 24, 28, 30, 39,
  51, 52, 53, 65, 70, 73, 75,
  92, 117, 132
Koop, Dr E. 119
Kuhse, Dr H. 52, 54, 55, 61,
  109, 124, 126, 128

Law 4, 13, 23, 27, 28, 32,
  34, 37, 39 et seq., 55, 57,
  109, 116
Law reform 4, 34, 39 et
  seq., 92, 114, 122 et seq.,
  127, 131, 133
Living will 94

Media 2, 62, 101
Medical profession 8, 10,
  11, 13, 15, 17, 23, 24, 29,
  44, 73, 75, 106, 108,
  110, 132
Mercy killing 20, 44, 107
Moral values 1, 4, 22, 25,
  26, 28, 29, 34, 35, 37, 52,
  62, 131
Morphine 87, 89
Murder 34, 39, 109

Netherlands League of
  Physicians 106
Newborn 5, 22, 51 et seq.,
  116 et seq.
Nurses 15, 16, 24, 44, 82,
  102

Obligations, see Duties
Opinion, public 42, 43, 48,
  59 et seq., 128, 129

Pain 9, 10, 16, 23, 65, 78,
  85 et seq., 88
Palliative care 4, 7 et seq.,
  18, 37, 44, 60, 66, 79, 82,
  107
Paraplegia 108, 115
Passive euthanasia 22 et
  seq., 106
Personhood 30, 53, 54,
  127
Philosophy 1, 25 et seq.,
  36, 51, 55, 65, 77, 98,
  120 et seq.
Power of attorney 94

Quadriplegia 98, 115

Raglan, Lord 46
Right to be killed 3, 33, 34,
  125
        to death with dignity
        33, 124

141

to die 3, 32, 33, 45,
    106
to kill 33
to life 33, 40
to painless dying 126
to refuse medical
    treatment 13, 33, 41,
    88, 94, 125
Rights 13, 27, 31 et seq.,
    40, 41, 55, 133
Royal Dutch Medical
    Association 106, 107

San Francisco Medical
    Society 128
Saunders, Dame C. 7
Self determination, see
    Autonomy
Singer, Prof P. 52, 61, 128
Smoker, B. 26
South Australia, Natural
    Death Act 33
Spina bifida 118
Suffering 18, 35, 36, 45, 64,
    79
Suicide 22, 39, 40, 107,
    112, 113
Symptom control 8

Teamwork 15
Technology, medical 2, 45,
    67, 79, 125
Twycross, Dr R. 90

United Kingdom 26, 44,
    45, 56, 89
United Nations
    Declarations of Rights
    40, 41, 127
    Human Rights
    Commission 124
United States 70, 80, 94,
    96, 97, 111, 113, 115,
    119, 122, 123
Uruguay 43
Utilitarianism 25 et seq.,
    51, 121

Victoria, Medical
    Treatment Act 33, 42
Victorian Law Reform
    Commission 44
Voluntary euthanasia 5, 21,
    36, 42, 47, 105, 112,
    114, 117

Williams, B. 121
Withdrawing treatment
    22, 23, 29
World Federation of Right
    to Die Societies 124
World Medical Association
    28